LEADER'S GUIDE

Dr. Mary Jo Osterman is a Christian educator who serves as a freelance writer and editor. A lifelong United Methodist currently living in Colorado, Dr. Osterman has written United Methodist curriculum materials and has led numerous workshops and leadership training events on a variety of issues. Dr. Osterman is the writer of the leader's guide for volume 10 of *Journey Through the Bible: Mark*.

---

1 AND 2 KINGS, 1 AND 2 CHRONICLES, EZRA, NEHEMIAH, ESTHER

Copyright © 1995 by Cokesbury
All rights reserved.

JOURNEY THROUGH THE BIBLE: 1 AND 2 KINGS, 1 AND 2 CHRONICLES, EZRA, NEHEMIAH, ESTHER: LEADER'S GUIDE. An official resource for The United Methodist Church prepared by the General Board of Discipleship through Church School Publications and published by Cokesbury, The United Methodist Publishing House; 201 Eighth Avenue, South; P.O. Box 801; Nashville, TN 37202-0801. Printed in the United States of America.

Scripture quotations in this publication, unless otherwise indicated, are from the New Revised Standard Version of the Bible, copyright ©1989 by the Division of Christian Education of the National Council of the Churches of Christ in the United States of America, and are used by permission. All rights reserved.

For permission to reproduce any material in this publication, call 615-749-6421, or write to Permissions Office, P.O. Box 801, Nashville, TN 37202-0801.

To order copies of this publication, call toll free 800-672-1789. Call Monday through Friday, 7:00–6:30 Central Time; 5:00–4:30 Pacific Time; Saturday, 9:00–5:00. You may FAX your order to 800-445-8189. Telecommunication Device for the Deaf/Telax Telephone: 800-227-4091. Automated order system is available after office hours. Use your Cokesbury account, American Express, Visa, Discover, or MasterCard.

EDITORIAL TEAM

Gary L. Ball-Kilbourne,
Editor

Norma L. Bates,
Assistant Editor

Linda O. Spicer,
Adult Section Assistant

DESIGN TEAM

Ed Wynne,
Layout Designer

Susan J. Scruggs,
*Design Supervisor,
Cover Design*

ADMINISTRATIVE STAFF

Neil M. Alexander,
Vice-President, Publishing

Duane A. Ewers,
Editor of Church School Publications

Gary L. Ball-Kilbourne,
Executive Editor of Adult Publications

THIS PUBLICATION IS PRINTED ON RECYCLED PAPER

Contents

Volume 5: 1 Kings—Esther by Mary Jo Osterman

Introduction to the Series		2
Chapter 1	Keep the Faith!	3
Chapter 2	Many Faces of Wisdom	8
Chapter 3	Folly and Downfall	13
Chapter 4	"My God Is Greater Than Yours!"	18
Chapter 5	Any Hope in Exile?	23
Chapter 6	New Occasions Bring New History	28
Chapter 7	Tragic Mistakes and New Beginnings	33
Chapter 8	A Second Chance	38
Chapter 9	Clean and Unclean	43
Chapter 10	Walls That Divide	48
Chapter 11	Two Women—Two Choices	53
Chapter 12	Upsetting the Balance	58
Chapter 13	"For Such a Time as This"	63
Two Histories of Israel		68
The First Audiences		70
Suggested Resource List		71
Chronology Chart for Kings Through Esther		72
Map: Great Empires of the Sixth Century B.C.		Inside Back Cover

Introduction to the Series

The leader's guides provided for use with JOURNEY THROUGH THE BIBLE make the following assumptions:

- adults learn in different ways:
  —by reading
  —by listening to speakers
  —by working on projects
  —by drama and roleplay
  —by using their imaginations
  —by expressing themselves creatively
  —by teaching others
- the mix of persons in your group is different from that found in any other group.
- the length of the actual time you have for teaching in a session may vary from thirty minutes to ninety minutes.
- the physical place where your class meets is not exactly like the place where any other group or class meets.
- your teaching skills, experiences, and preferences are unlike anyone else's.

We encourage you to discover and develop the ways you can best use the information and learning ideas in this leader's guide with your particular class. To get started, we suggest you try following these steps:

1. Think and pray about your individual class members. Who are they? What are they like? Why are they involved in this particular Bible study class at this particular time in their lives? What seem to be their needs? How do you think they learn best?
2. Think and pray about your class members as a group. A group takes on a character that can be different from the particular characters of the individuals who make up that group. How do your class members interact? What do they enjoy doing together? What would help them become stronger as a group?
3. Keep in mind that you are teaching this class for the sake of the class members, in order to help them increase in their faithfulness as disciples of Jesus Christ. Teachers sometimes fall prey to the danger of teaching in ways that are easiest for themselves. The best teachers accept the discomfort of taking risks and stretching their teaching skills in order to focus on what will really help the class members learn and grow in their faith.
4. Read the chapter in the study book. Read the assigned Bible passages. Read the background Bible passages, if any. Work through the Dimension 1 questions in the study book. Make a list of any items you do not understand and need to research further using such tools as Bible dictionaries, concordances, Bible atlases, and commentaries. In other words, do your homework. Be prepared with your own knowledge about the Bible passages being studied by your class.
5. Read the chapter's material in the leader's guide. You might want to begin with the "Additional Bible Helps," found at the *end* of each chapter. Then look at each learning idea in the "Learning Menu."
6. Spend some time with the "Learning Menu." Notice that the "Learning Menu" is organized around Dimensions 1, 2, and 3 in the study book. Recognizing that different adults and adult classes will learn best using different teaching/learning methods, in each of the three dimensions you will find
   —at least one learning idea that is primarily discussion-based;
   —at least one learning idea that begins with a method other than discussion, but which may lead into discussion.
   Make notes about which learning ideas will work best given the unique makeup and setting of your class.
7. Decide on a lesson plan. Which learning ideas will you lead the class members through when? What materials will you need? What other preparations do you need to make? How long do you plan to spend on a particular learning idea?
8. Many experienced teachers have found that they do better if they plan more than they actually use during a class session. They also know that their class members may become frustrated if they try to do too much during a class session. In other words
   —plan more than you can actually use. That way, you have back-up learning ideas in case something does not work well or something takes much less time than you thought.
   —don't try to do everything listed in the "Learning Menu." We have intentionally offered you much more than you can use in one class session.
   —be flexible while you teach. A good lesson plan is only a guide for your use as you teach people. Keep the focus on your class members, not your lesson plan.
9. After you teach, evaluate the class session. What worked well? What did not? What did you learn from your experience of teaching that will help you plan for the next class session?

May God's Spirit be upon you as you lead your class on their *Journey Through the Bible!*

Questions or comments? Call Curric-U-Phone 1-800-251-8591.

1

1 Kings 2:1-4; 3:5-15

Keep the Faith!

LEARNING MENU

Keeping in mind the ways in which your class members learn best as well as their needs and interests, choose at least one learning segment from each of the three Dimensions. Each Dimension offers discussion and hands-on type activities. You may want to do at least one hands-on type activity. If class members arrive at staggered times, you may want to offer several Dimension 1 activities as choices as they arrive.

Opening Prayer

This prayer might be used at the beginning of each session:

Gracious and loving God, open our hearts and minds as we begin (continue) this study. Help us to discern your living word within the stories of Israel's journey. Amen.

Dimension 1: What Does the Bible Say?

(A) Play an outline card game.

This activity will help class members recall the books of the Bible and put this Kings to Esther study into the larger context.

- Before class time, write on 4x6 index cards the names of each of the books of the Old Testament from Genesis through Esther (twelve cards, one book to a card). Make two more cards (on a different color card or with a different color ink) that say: "Primary Biblical History from Creation to Babylonian Exile," and "Secondary Biblical History from Creation to Persian Rule." Have available a copy of the article on page 68 of this leader's guide, "Two Histories of Israel."

- As the session starts, mix up the cards and give them to persons to sort. Ask them first to put the books of the Bible in the right order. Encourage them to consult their Bibles. When they have ordered the cards, they will discover the two summary cards left over. Ask them to group the books of the Bible under each of these two summary cards. The article on page 68 will help them figure out why these two cards refer to two different types of biblical history.

- Additional background information may be found in David J. A. Clines's article, "Introduction to the Biblical Story: Genesis—Esther," in *Harper's Bible Commentary* (HarperSanFrancisco, 1988; pages 74–84).

- Conclude this activity by pointing out that in this unit you will be studying the end of the primary history and all of the secondary history.

(B) Start a timeline.

- You will need a long roll of butcher paper (or a ball of twine, clothespins, and 4x6 index cards) and felt-tip markers. Also have ready a Bible dictionary or a copy of the timeline from *Bible Teacher Kit* (Abingdon Press, 1994; available from Cokesbury).
- Ask class members to put the following items on the timeline, along with the appropriate dates:
—Abraham and Sarah leave Ur
—Joseph arrives as a slave in Egypt
—Moses/Miriam lead Exodus out of Egypt
—Judges lead the people of Israel
—Samuel is a prophet who assumed national leadership
—Saul reigns as first king
—David becomes king
- Be sure to leave space on the timeline to add items in later sessions.

(C) Be a Bible researcher.

- Collect a Bible dictionary, a Bible commentary or two (see "Suggested Resource List," page 71), and a copy of the article, "Stories Within Stories in Kings" on page 6.
- Ask a team to prepare a short report to share with the whole class, using the following research questions:
  1. How many centuries does First and Second Kings cover?
  2. What "written sources" did the storyteller use to put together his version of the history of the kings? What kinds of "sources" did he mention that he drew on? What other sources did he probably use?
  Clues: Look up "First and Second Kings" and then look for subheadings such as "Historical Background," "Sources," or "Literary History."

(D) Review questions in study book.

- For this first session, give class members time to answer the questions in their study books. Urge them to read the study book and answer the questions in Dimension 1 before coming to class next time.
- Share and check answers as a whole class. Do this as quickly as possible before moving to Dimension 2 and 3 activities, which are the "meat" of the session.
- Suggested answers:
  1. The dying King David charges his son Solomon to "keep the charge of the LORD your God." Solomon is to keep the faith. He is to keep God's laws as they have been set forth in Deuteronomy ("the law of Moses"), the main thrust of which is to love and worship the LORD exclusively.
  2. If Solomon "keeps the charge of the LORD" he will prosper in everything he does as king and he will ensure that there will always be an heir for the Davidic throne of Israel. That is, the monarchy will survive and prosper.
  3. In Solomon's dream at the high holy place of Gibeon, he dreams that he asks God for wisdom so that he might govern the people of Israel well.
  4. God responds by giving Solomon the wisdom he asks for, plus the wealth and fame that he did not ask for.

Dimension 2: What Does the Bible Mean?

(E) Provide a mini-lecture on the first audiences of the Book of Kings.

- Help your class members get clearly in mind who the storyteller and the audience are. Use the articles "Who Was the Storyteller?" page 7, and "The Audience of the Deuteronomistic Storytellers," page 70, as background material for developing a mini-lecture. An outline for a mini-lecture is provided below.
- Say, "All through this study of Kings to Esther, we will be moving back and forth between the actual stories of the kings and the perspective and motives of the later storyteller of Kings."
- Then continue your mini-lecture covering these points:
—Who the storyteller was
—Who the first audiences were
—How the audiences felt about exile
—What the storyteller expected of them

> **HOW TO DO A MINI-LECTURE**
> Use a chalkboard, markerboard, or newsprint to list each of your main points as you make them. Or before class, print your main points on newsprint—each point on a separate page. Put up or display one sheet at a time as you deliver the mini-lecture. Using the newsprint or board will give class members a visual reminder while you are verbally telling them about the three audiences. Hearing and seeing will greatly increase what class members remember from your lecture.

(F) Find the storyteller's "formula."

- Introduce this activity by saying: "The storyteller of Kings has a pattern by which he introduces each king, evaluates his reign, and then closes out that king's story."
- Look first at one example: Solomon and Rehoboam in 1 Kings 11:41-43; 14:21-22, 29-31. Ask class members to identify the various parts of this formula. (See information in box on page 5 for more help.) If you have time, ask class members to look through later parts of First or Second Kings to find the pattern for other kings.

- Conclude this activity by noting: "This pattern in the storytelling is one of the identifying traits of the Deuteronomistic historian storyteller of Kings. It is one of the keys to understanding the 'bias' of this storyteller."

> **THE STORYTELLER'S FORMULA**
>
> With few exceptions the Deuteronomistic historian, the storyteller, uses a set formula to introduce each king, evaluate his reign, and close out his story.
>
> Using Solomon's death and Rehoboam's succession we can see the pattern:
> - 1 Kings 11:41-43: The death of one king is noted by the standard phrase, "Now the rest of the acts of [king's name], are they not written in [name of a book]" and by the phrase "slept with his ancestors." The dying king's length of reign is sometimes noted, and his successor is named.
> - 1 Kings 14:21: The next king is noted by how old he was when he began to rule and by how long he ruled. Often his mother's name is reported. Sometimes this statement follows immediately after the death notation, and sometimes it comes later in the story, as in the case of Rehoboam.
> - 1 Kings 14:22: The ruling king is evaluated by the phrase that he was/did "evil in the sight of the LORD." This evaluation statement comes somewhere in the storyteller's description of the king's activities.

(G) Identify traits of a wise king.

- On board or newsprint list class members' ideas about what a "wise king" was in David and Solomon's day.
- Ask them to read 1 Kings 2:1-4 and 3:5-15. Ask for further traits to add to the list.
- Finally, ask half the class members to look up Deuteronomy 17:14-20 and half to look up Isaiah 11:2-5, which describe the ideal king of Israel. Add more traits to the list.
- Discussion questions:
  1. What observations can you make about this list of traits of a wise king of Israel that we have just developed?
  2. From what you remember about your past study of David, did he live up to this list of traits of the wise king?

(H) Visualize the political succession of Solomon.

- Invite class members to get comfortable for a guided visualization activity about the succession of Solomon to the throne. (Some may want to close their eyes, others may want to sit on the floor or take some other kind of meditation pose.)
- Use the following visualization, reading the words in italics slowly. Pause wherever there is a series of dots to give students time to think and feel.

  Take a deep breath and let it out very slowly; . . . breathe slowly in and out; . . . let your body relax and your mind become still. . . .

  Imagine yourself back into history, . . . back before the Civil War, . . . before the American Revolution, . . . before the time of Martin Luther and the Reformation, . . . before the time of Jesus, . . . way back into history to the time of King David in Israel. . . .

  Imagine that you are Queen Bathsheba, and you are watching the servants scurrying back and forth to the king's rooms; . . . you are watching from a darkened hallway when they bring the beautiful young maiden, Abishag, to your husband; . . . you know the king is ailing and you wonder what will happen; . . . you have heard rumors that David's son Adonijah has gathered supporters around him, waiting and watching. You know that if Adonijah becomes king you and your son Solomon will be in danger. . . .

  What are you thinking? . . . How do you feel? . . . What can you do? . . . .

  Imagine now that you are David's son Adonijah; . . . you are the oldest living son; . . . common sense says that you should be the next king, . . . but you have also heard that Solomon wants to be king and that Bathsheba and the prophet Nathan are supporting him; . . . well, so what! You have supporters too and they will help you; . . . in fact they already have; . . . I will declare myself king before Solomon thinks about it! . . .

  What are your thoughts and feelings as you make the preparations? . . . .

  Imagine now that you are the prophet Nathan; . . . you have been with King David a long, long time; . . . you remember back when David was young and foolish; . . . you remember how David had Bathsheba's husband Uriah killed so he could have her as a wife. . . . Remember how hard you were on David's folly? . . . You spoke the LORD's judgment then; . . . but what must you do now? . . . Adonijah is making moves to become king; . . . it feels like a repeat of Absalom's plans to take over David's throne. . . . Is this what the LORD wants? Or is it Solomon? When David was so foolish with Bathsheba and the baby died; . . . when another baby was born, the LORD was pleased and the baby Solomon was called "Beloved of the Lord";

  . . . that must be the LORD's wish; . . . you must find Bathsheba and make plans. . . .

  What are you thinking? . . . How are you feeling? . . . . .

  Slowly now bring yourself back down through the centuries to the present. . . . When you are ready, open your eyes and quietly rejoin the class.

- When all are ready, ask class members to reflect on the guided visualization: how did they feel as Bathsheba? as

Adonijah? as Nathan? Guide them to share feelings they think the characters might have had as well as thoughts.
- Note with class members that they were not guided to think about Solomon. Solomon was really in the background. Talk about what he might have thought and how he might have felt.
- Ask for any general understandings class members gained about the biblical story.

Dimension 3: What Does the Bible Mean to Us?

(I) Explore the storyteller's bias.

- Introduce this activity by sharing the following thoughts: "The first listeners to the storyteller of Kings may have experienced their new storyteller in the same way that we experience a new storyteller who writes about our religious leaders like Paul, Martin Luther, John Wesley, Cotton Mather, and Billy Graham. We may know the leaders and their factual stories; but a new storyteller provides us with fresh clues about the meanings and the consequences of those leaders' beliefs and actions."
- Invite class membes to share at this point what they think the bias is of the storyteller of Kings. Get out the ideas, but urge them to keep an open mind and to keep watching during the next four sessions.
- Explore the question from the study book: "Do we believe this storyteller's claim that God directly guides all events of history?" Look at the other questions raised at the end of Dimension 3 in the study book. Suggest that class members watch for this claim and keep thinking about their own understandings.

(J) Reflect on how you are a wise leader.

- Provide paper and pencils, and invite class members individually to reflect on how and where they personally serve as a leader. Suggest that they write a modern prayer asking God for whatever it is that they need to be a leader in their own situation.
- Some persons may want to share thoughts or the prayer they wrote, but do not press everyone to share.

(K) Imagine the ideal leader.

- Divide class members into two groups: one group is to imagine the ideal national leader and the other group, the ideal religious leader. Put aside all "real" limitations like titles of President and Bishop or two-party political systems. Create the image of each leader as imaginatively as possible.
- Once the two teams have their "leader" well defined, ask them to pick one person from their team to "play" that person. The two "leaders" come together to try to solve the global problem of ongoing small-scale wars over land ownership between ethnic, tribal, and religious groups like the ones that have occurred off and on over centuries in the Middle East. (If this problem will not work for your class, pick another major global problem like ending poverty, ending hunger, or curbing overpopulation.)
- Get the two leaders started talking by asking each one to make an opening statement about their views on the problem. Encourage them to talk to each other and to engage in problem-solving behaviors based on the traits their teams gave them as ideal leaders.
- When the conversation is going well between the two, stop it. (The class will feel much more successful that way than if you let the dialogue die out with actors not knowing what to do next.)
- Ask class members to comment on the wise leader traits they saw in each leader. If you have time, encourage teams to coach their leader, and then do a second conversation between the leaders who are still trying to solve the same problem. Again, cut the conversation at a high point and ask for further reflections and insights about wise leadership patterns in national and religious leaders in our century.

Closing Prayer

God of change and glory, God of time and space, we give you thanks for your ongoing love and concern for us. We give you thanks for new insights into the Bible stories of the past. We confess we are not always comfortable with new ideas and new ways of looking at our faith, but we continue to seek more understanding of you that we might better worship and praise you. Amen.

Additional Bible Helps

Stories Within Stories in Kings
The story of Kings is about the actual time of David, Solomon, and the other kings of Israel and Judah. These monarchs lived from 961 B.C. (when David died) to the fall of Jerusalem in 587/586 B.C. The actual history of the kings was first gathered into early separate sagas or documents. One early saga is the "court history" of David's reign. Another early saga is a "succession narrative" that tells about the rise of Solomon and the demise of his brother and enemies. A third early story is made up of old "prophetic legends and miracle stories" written in the Northern Kingdom before it fell. A fourth early document can be identified as "temple archives."

Some of these early stories and documents probably were later included in three books the storyteller of Kings mentions: "Book of the Acts of Solomon" (1 Kings

11:41); "Books of the Annals [or Chronicles] of the Kings of Israel" (1 Kings 14:19); "Books of the Annals of the Kings of Judah" (1 Kings 14:29). Those three books have been lost.

The storyteller may have written an early version of Kings as a national history of the Northern Kingdom. If so, this Deuteronomistic storyteller would have written his version before the fall of Samaria in 721 B.C. Another Deuteronomistic storyteller may have written a second version of Kings during the reign of King Josiah (about 620 B.C.) in Judah. The version we have of First and Second Kings was written by a Deuteronomistic storyteller after Jerusalem fell in 587/586 B.C. He wrote from exile in Babylonia to the exiled peoples who were experiencing a crisis of faith.

Who Was the Storyteller?
The storyteller of First and Second Kings was a writer, a historian of sorts, an editor, and a preacher with a major theological point to make. The storyteller was not a single person, but rather a group of people whom biblical scholars have named the Deuteronomistic historian. This group of people edited and shaped the material that we now have in the books of Deuteronomy, Joshua, Judges, First and Second Samuel, and First and Second Kings. They wrote over a period of time, though scholars disagree both on dates and on how many versions of Israel's history they wrote.

One theory is that the first Deuteronomistic writers were a group of prophets or priests living in Jerusalem during the early part of Josiah's reign (about 650–640 B.C.). They collected the ancient Mosiac laws and traditions into an early form of the Book of Deuteronomy. It was probably that book that the high priest Hilkiah (hil-KIGH-uh) "found" in the Temple in the eighteenth year of Josiah's reign (about 621 B.C.).

Other scholars do not believe this early version existed. They believe the Deuteronomistic writers lived during the Exile in Babylonia and wrote their history there.

No matter which theory is accepted, scholars identify the seven books of Deuteronomy through Second Kings as the Deuteronomistic history of Israel. It is called "Deuteronomistic" because the writers used the core of laws in Deuteronomy to explain Israel's history and to judge Israel's kings and Israel's people. Deuteronomistic writers explained that Israel's abandonment of faith in the LORD led to the downfall of the monarchy and the exile of the people. Besides explaining the suffering of the exiled peoples, the writers were also telling the exiled people to change their ways in order to gain God's support again.

2
1 Kings 3:16-28; 5:1-18; 8:1-21

Many Faces of Wisdom

LEARNING MENU

Keeping in mind the ways in which your class members learn best as well as their needs and interests, choose at least one learning segment from each of the three Dimensions. Each Dimension offers both discussion and more active kinds of activities. You might want to invite different class members to work on activities "A," "B," and "C" as they arrive in the classroom.

Dimension 1: What Does the Bible Say?

(A) Identify Tyre on a map.

- Before the class session hang a large map of Solomon's united kingdom. (See "The United Monarchy" wall map in *Bible Teacher Kit* [Abingdon, 1994; available from Cokesbury], find one in the teaching files in your Sunday school, or use the map on page 9 of the study book.) Provide a Bible dictionary, a sheet of colored construction paper, scissors, and tape or thumb tacks.
- Ask some class members to find the city of Tyre and the city of Jerusalem and to mark them with big paper arrows. Using a Bible dictionary, look up *Hiram of Tyre* and *trade* to learn more about the relationship Solomon probably had with Hiram and other neighbors. Ask this team to prepare a short report for the whole class.

(B) Add to the timeline.

- Ask class members to find approximate dates for the building of Solomon's Temple (see 1 Kings 6:1, 37), and add "Solomon Builds the Temple" to the timeline.

(C) Research the Temple.

- Try to find one or two old "teaching pictures" from the children's Sunday school materials showing the inside and outside of Solomon's Temple. Hang these in the area where a team will be working.
- Ask some class members to use Bible dictionaries to learn about Solomon's Temple. Also, refer them to material in the study book (pages 16–17). Ask them to be prepared to give a short report to the whole class.

(D) Discover different interpretations of the prostitute's tale.

- Provide several commentaries on Kings (such as *Harper's Bible Commentary*; *The Women's Bible Com-*

8   JOURNEY THROUGH THE BIBLE

mentary; First and Second Kings: Interpretation: A Bible Commentary for Teaching and Preaching, by Richard Nelson; *The Interpreter's Bible*; *The New Interpreter's Bible*, when available). Also provide a copy of the background article "Similar Folktales of Two Mothers" ("Additional Bible Helps," page 11).

- Ask class members to look up 1 Kings 3:16-28, the story of Solomon, two women, and a baby, in the commentaries.
- Class members might also look up the passage in several different translations to find different words and phrases used by translators.
- Find out:
  1. What points does each commentary make about the story? Are the commentators all saying the same things, or do they have different points of view?
  2. What does each commentator say about similar tales outside biblical literature?
- Ask class members to share their learnings with the whole class when you do activity "F."

(E) Review the Dimension 1 questions in the study book.

- If some people have not read the study book material and answered Dimension 1 questions, invite them to do so while others are engaged in activities "A," "B," "C," or "D."
- When all are ready, quickly review the questions to be sure class members have found the answers.
- Suggested answers:
  1. Solomon's "wise" advice is to cut the living baby in half, thus giving each woman half, since each claims it is her baby.
  2. Solomon reaffirms the treaty King Hiram had with David. They agree that Hiram will provide building materials and craftsmen to help Solomon build a temple for the LORD in Jerusalem. This was partly an economic agreement; Solomon needed the building supplies and workers. It was also probably a "peace treaty" to keep relationships friendly.
  3. David had wanted to build a temple for the LORD. But God promised David that his son would build a temple. Solomon is the son who fulfills that promise.

Dimension 2: What Does the Bible Mean?

(F) Discuss meanings of the prostitute story.

- If class members did activity "D," invite them to share their learnings as you discuss the following questions.

  1. What difference does it make in the story that the two women are prostitutes?
  2. Does the explanation given about how the child died make sense to you?
  3. Why would the mother of the dead child do what she did?
  4. Which mother is speaking to Solomon? Can we be sure?

(G) Discuss meanings of Solomon's administration of the monarchy.

- If class members did activity "A," ask them to give a short report. Then engage the whole class in the following discussion.
- Questions:
  1. What might have happened if Solomon had not renewed the treaty with King Hiram of Tyre that his father, David, had first made?
  2. What benefits did Hiram and Solomon each get from the treaty or trade agreement? (See 1 Kings 9:10-14 in addition to 1 Kings 5.)
  3. Who were the "losers" in this treaty?
  4. What are the other administrative actions that Solomon took early in his reign? (See 1 Kings 4.) Who were the winners and losers of these agreements?
  5. There is no mention of women in all these agreements. Can you draw any tentative conclusions about how Hebrew women fared in all these treaties and royal administrative activities? What about non-Hebrew women?

(H) Create two imaginary conversations.

- Ask class members to write an imaginary conversation. Give them two choices:
  1. a conversation between King Hiram and Solomon as they renew the treaty that King Hiram had originally made with Solomon's father, David;
  2. a conversation between the grieving prostitute and a bystander in the court after Solomon's decision.
- Set a time limit for their writing, based on what else you want to do during the class time. At the end of the time, stop people even if they are not finished and ask for one example of each conversation. Let class members respond with comments to the writer. Encourage people to finish writing the conversations at home if they wish.
- If you have more time: Have more class members read their conversations.
- If you have less time: Instead of reading conversations, ask class members: What insights did you gain from doing these conversations?

(I) Experience a dramatic reading about the Temple.

- Before class time: Ask two members of the class to be prepared to read dramatically 1 Kings 8 to the other class members. One should read the parts that Solomon says; the other will be the narrator and read the descriptive parts, including the lead-in phrases like "Then Solomon said" or "He said."
- Choose two good readers and encourage them to practice ahead of time and to read the part expressively as if they were addressing a large worshiping congregation.
- In class: Ask class members to make themselves comfortable and to close their eyes if they wish while the two class members read the story of the dedication of the Temple.
- After the reading, ask class members for both feelings and thoughts or ideas about what the dedication of the Temple probably meant to those who were there.

(J) Imagine the first listeners' feelings.

- Review quickly the four audiences of the storyteller of Kings. (See "The Audience of the Deuteronomistic Storytellers," page 70.) Divide class members into four teams. Each team becomes one of the four audiences. Raise the following questions one at the time with them. Let each "audience team" respond to question 1 before you go on to question 2 and then question 3. Encourage them to respond as if they really were that long-ago audience.
  1. You have just heard the storyteller tell the tale about Solomon and the two prostitute mothers. What kinds of feelings do you have listening to this storyteller of the kings tell about Solomon's wisdom with the two prostitutes?
  2. You have just listened to the storyteller's tale of Solomon and King Hiram. How do you feel about Solomon's "wise" administrative decisions with King Hiram and his use of forced labor to build the Temple in Jerusalem?
  3. Here you are listening to a storyteller describe the most magnificent thing that ever happened in Israel, the dedication of God's Temple, an event that happened three hundred to four hundred years before you lived. Now the Temple is in ruins. What kinds of positive feelings do you have? what kinds of negative ones?
- After discussing these questions "in character as the long-ago audience," invite class members to come back into the present. Ask them to share any new insights they got about those long-ago audiences and about the storyteller's motives for retelling those particular stories.

Dimension 3: What Does the Bible Mean to Us?

(K) Discuss the meaning of *wisdom*.

- Provide a modern dictionary. Ask someone to look up the word *wisdom* and to read the various definitions. (Note: Dictionaries tend to offer two different kinds of definitions of *wisdom* as it is used today: 1. accumulated philosophic or scientific learning or knowledge; and 2. insight; good sense; good judgment; a wise attitude or course of action.)
- Ask the class members: "Which definition fits our understanding of Solomon's wisdom? What other words or phrases would you add to the dictionary definition in order to define Solomon's kinds of wisdom for today?"

(L) Explore stereotypes and wisdom.

- Tell class members: "Someone in Solomon's time, who was less wise than Solomon, might have said: 'Both women are prostitutes, and prostitutes are strangers full of lies. The baby probably does not belong to either of them. Let us take it away and give it to a "proper" mother.' This would probably have been the conventional wisdom of the time."
  1. What stereotypes exist in that conventional way of solving the dilemma of the two prostitutes?
  2. Do we lay similar stereotypes on prostitutes today? Or do we have different stereotypes of prostitutes today?
  3. What stereotypes do we lay on other groups of people today that make them "strangers full of lies and folly" whom we can then easily ignore and dismiss? What groups? What stereotypes?
  4. What might a wise leader say or do today to break through those stereotypes?

(M) Explore a modern administrative situation.

- Before class time: Print the questions below in large letters on newsprint, chalkboard, or markerboard so they can be read from various parts of the classroom. Or make enough copies of the questions to hand one set to each team.
- Divide class members into teams of three. Ask each team to pick one of the following modern situations: a pastor/administrative board, a mayor/city council, a governor/legislature, a president/Congress. It would help but is not absolutely necessary for different teams to choose different situations. Ask each team to discuss the following questions (which you have printed on the board, on newsprint, or copied on handouts ahead of time).

1. What kinds of administrative decisions have been made in your situation? Who made them? Who enforces them?
2. Who are the "winners" of these administrative decisions? How? Why?
3. Who are the "losers"? How? Why? How have they responded to the inequities in the situation?
4. What changes would have to be made to make this situation more equal for everyone?
5. What and who would be the "barriers" to any such proposed changes toward more equality in your situation?
6. How might those barriers be overcome?
7. Does our study of Solomon's ways provide any insight in what to do and not to do in "wise administration"?

(N) Discuss modern implications of Solomon's wisdom.

- Use the various questions below to discuss the material in Dimension 3 in the study book:
  1. Do our leaders today exhibit wisdom in their judicial, administrative, and religious decisions? What evidence can you give that they do? that they do not? How do you explain the fights, stalling, and pork barrel deals in Congress and the special interest lobby groups? Are these God's ways of wisdom?
  2. Do we ourselves exhibit wisdom when we are in a position of leadership?
  3. Are our tax districts and taxes any fairer than Solomon's?
  4. Are our labor laws in harmony with God's ways? What about our international trade agreements?

(O) Reflect on your own wisdom and leadership.

- You will need paper and pencils or pens for everyone to use.
- Invite participants to reflect privately on their understandings of "wisdom" and "wise leadership" for their lives today. Encourage them also to write about how their understandings and leadership decisions impact a much larger circle of people and institutions.
- Check with people as they finish to see if any would like to share one or two thoughts they had.

(P) Create an image of wisdom.

- You will need paints and paper, or felt-tip markers and drawing paper.
- Invite class members to create a visual image of wisdom. Remind them of the different kinds of wisdom we saw in Solomon's reign: judicial, administrative, and religious wisdom. Ask them to come up with one symbol, or an interrelated set of three symbols for wisdom that would mean something to people today. Offer examples of other symbols we have today: a set of scales to symbolize justice; a dove to symbolize peace.

TEACHING TIP
If you think class members will not "draw"
Adults often think they cannot "draw" so they are reluctant to try an activity like activity "P." Encourage them to do more abstract or symbolic types of art rather than realistic drawings. The color of paint or marker they use might be part of the symbol. The boldness or thinness of a line might help convey their idea. Keep telling them that they do not have to "draw." All they have to do is get their idea out some way. Do a symbol yourself as they work. Keep encouraging them!

- Ask those who want to, to share their symbols and say a little about them. Give lots of praise for the ideas and images they share!
- If you have wall space, consider grouping the class members' symbols attractively and add a large printed heading: SYMBOLS OF WISDOM FOR TODAY.

Additional Bible Helps

Similar Folktales of Two Mothers
No one knows whether the two prostitutes were real people who actually approached Solomon with their dilemma or whether this is a folktale told by the storyteller of Kings to make a point about Solomon. We do know, however, that this kind of story shows up many times in ancient world folklore. Scholars have collected over twenty-two different samples of ancient stories in which a wise judge orders the cutting in two of a child being fought over.

Harper's Bible Commentary notes that the most similar story in ancient literature is "a Jain tale of two women, widows of the same man, who claim to be the mother of his child and, therefore, the rightful head of his household and heir to his estate." Like Solomon, a magistrate orders the child be divided. The true mother in this tale, as in the tale of the prostitutes, quickly gives up her claims to the child and the estate. She pleads for the child's life. Like Solomon, the magistrate awards the child to that woman. He also awards her the estate (from *Harper's Bible Commentary*, James L. Mays, general editor; Harper & Row, 1988; page 309).

King Hiram of Tyre
Hiram was the king of Tyre, a city-state on the Mediterranean coast west of northern Israel. A contemporary of David and Solomon, he built his kingdom into a great empire, which he ruled for thirty-four years (969–935 B.C.). He was nineteen years old when he began to rule.

The storyteller of Kings gives us a little description of Hiram's kingdom during David's and Solomon's times. Under Hiram's rule, and with David's help, the Philistines who controlled the coastline were subdued and the city of Tyre became the greatest city on the Phoenician coast. Hiram aided Solomon with building materials and craftsmen to build the Temple in Jerusalem. Solomon supplied Hiram with wheat and olive oil (1 Kings 5). Later Hiram gave Solomon gold and more building materials in exchange for twenty towns in Galilee known together as Cabul (KAY-buhl, 1 Kings 9:10-13). Hiram also helped Solomon with his trading adventures by supplying ships and sailors (1 Kings 9:26-28).

The Structure of Kings
We can look at the larger structure of the Book of Kings in two different ways. First, we can see what is contained in the two books as we have them today:

First Kings
   The first book of Kings tells the story of Israel's history from the death of David in 961 B.C. to the death of Ahab and succession of Ahaziah (ay-huh-ZIGH-uh) in 850 B.C.

Second Kings
   The second book of Kings continues the story of Ahaziah through the fall of Samaria in 722/721 to the fall of Jerusalem in 587/586 B.C.

A second, more realistic and helpful way to look at the structure of Kings is to see it as a story with three divisions, rather than as two books. Together these three divisions cover the monarchy over a period of four hundred years:

1 Kings 1–11—The United Monarchy
   This section continues the story from Second Samuel, including the death of David, the reign of Solomon, and the building of the Temple.

1 Kings 12–2 Kings 17—The Divided Monarchy
   This section describes the revolt of the northern tribes and the founding of the Northern Kingdom of Israel by Jeroboam. It alternates between stories of the kings of the northern and southern kingdoms. It continues to the fall of Samaria and the destruction of the Northern Kingdom.

2 Kings 18–25—The Divided Monarchy: South
   This section describes the last days of Judah, including the two faithful kings, Hezekiah (hez-uh-KIGH-uh) and Josiah (joh-SIGH-uh), who tried to institute religious reforms that would return their people to the ancient ways of worshiping the LORD.

3 Folly and Downfall

1 Kings 11:9-13, 41-43; 12:1-33

LEARNING MENU

Keeping in mind the ways in which your class members learn best as well as their needs and interests, choose at least one learning segment from each of the three Dimensions. Each Dimension offers both discussion and more active, hands-on type activities. You might want to consider doing at least one active type activity in this session.

Dimension 1: What Does the Bible Say?

(A) Identify the divided monarchy on a map.

- You will need two different colored balls of yarn (bright colors that will show off against the wall map you put up last week. If you did not do Activity "A" last week, you will need a large map of "The United Monarchy" for this activity), colored construction paper, scissors, and straight pins.
- Invite early arriving persons to study the map of "The Kingdoms of Israel and Judah" in their study books (page 25) to identify the boundaries of the northern and southern kingdoms. Have them use yarn and pins to "outline" the boundaries of the Northern Kingdom in one color and the Southern Kingdom in another color. Make an arrow and write *Shechem* on it. Place the arrow on the map. If Jerusalem was not marked last week with an arrow, have class members do so today.

(B) Add to the wall timeline.

- Invite class members to add the closing date of Solomon's reign to the timeline, if your class did Activity "B" for sessions 1 and 2. Then add Rehoboam's name and the dates of his reign over Judah and Jeroboam's name and the dates of his reign over Israel. Class members may find dates by looking up both names in a Bible dictionary or by using the chronology chart in this leader's guide, page 72. Note: the dates of Rehoboam's reign are not specifically known. Various scholars propose dates from 937 to 922 as the beginning of his reign.

(C) Find out about Jeroboam and Rehoboam.

- Invite class members to look up *Jeroboam* and *Rehoboam* in a Bible dictionary. Ask them to find out:

1. Which one was Solomon's son? Who was this man's mother?
2. How was the other man connected to Solomon? What was his tribal heritage?

- Ask class members to be prepared to give a very short report on the two kings.

(D) Look up the Deuteronomy worship laws.

- Provide a Bible dictionary (*Harper's Bible Dictionary* if possible; see "Suggested Resource List," page 71) and "Israelite Worship: Visions, Practices, and Reforms" ("Additional Bible Helps," page 16).
- Invite class members to explore the nature of worship in ancient Israel. Look up *worship* in the Bible dictionary. Read the section from this leader's guide.
- Prepare a short report on Israelite worship: its ideal, its real practices, and the changes and reforms that actually took place over hundreds of years.

(E) Review the questions in the study book.

- If class members have not read the study book and answered Dimension 1 questions, give them time at the beginning of the session to complete this part of the lesson. Members who have already done this work can be encouraged to do one or more of activities "A," "B," "C," and "D."
- Review the questions and answers quickly with the class members, and move on to the other parts of the lesson in Dimensions 2 and 3.
- Suggested answers:
  1. The storyteller of the Book of Kings judges Solomon very negatively: Solomon's "heart has turned away from the LORD, the God of Israel." The LORD, says the storyteller, is very angry with Solomon and will destroy Solomon's monarchy.
  2. The people of the northern tribes probably were angry and resentful of Solomon's forced labor levy and his heavy taxes. Also, his twelve new administrative districts ignored the old tribal boundaries that the people may have preferred.
  3. Rehoboam's tragic mistake was that he listened to his young advisors instead of his older ones. He refused to lighten the burdens of forced labor and heavy taxes on the people of the northern tribes.
  4. Jeroboam's folly is that he introduces changes in worship practices into the lives of his people in the Northern Kingdom.

Dimension 2: What Does the Bible Mean?

(F) Discuss the actions of Rehoboam and Jeroboam.

- Engage all the class members in a short discussion time. If some members have reports from activities "C" and "D," invite them to share during the discussion. Use the following questions as starters:
  1. Why does Solomon's united monarchy divide? Explore both the human mistake of Rehoboam (in 12:1-15) and the divine reasons laid out by the storyteller (in 11:9-13).
  2. Who are these two new kings, Rehoboam and Jeroboam? (If class members did Activity "C," they can give their report here.)
  3. Why does Jeroboam introduce changes into the worship practices of the people in the new Northern Kingdom? Why are these viewed so negatively by the storyteller? (If class members did a report from activity "D," they can share here.)
  4. Who would you say is the "oppressor" king and who the "liberator" king? What evidence can you point to in the biblical passage to support your answer?

(G) Create a conversation between advisors.

- Divide the class members into two teams, one on one side of the room, one on the other side. One team represents Rehoboam's older advisors; the other his younger advisors.
- Set the stage: Read to the whole class 1 Kings 12:3-5. (The *they* in verse 3 refers to the people of the northern tribes.)
- Invite each team to look at the relevant verses: older advisors (12:6-8) and younger advisors (12:8-11). To do this quickly, have one person in each team read the verses aloud to his or her team. Each team should briefly talk as a team about what their verses mean.
- Invite the dialogue: Ask the two sets of advisors to face each other and talk with each other in character. Why should Rehoboam follow their advice rather than the other advisors' advice?
- Stop the dialogue when it is going strong. Ask everyone to come back into the present and be themselves.
- Then ask:
  1. What did you learn about your advisors?
  2. What did you learn about the other advisors?
  3. Knowing that Rehoboam took the advice of the younger advisors, what have you learned about Rehoboam?

(H) Write a monologue for Jeroboam.

- Invite class members to write out an expansion of the conversation Jeroboam had with himself in 1 Kings 12:26-27. Encourage them to write as if they were Jeroboam, expressing his fears about Rehoboam, his fears about his people's loyalties, his concerns about making worship changes, his explanations for the changes that are described in verses 28-33.
- Invite some members to share their written monologues if they wish. Then ask: what insights have you gained about Israel's struggle with worship practices?
- Another way: If your class members do not like to write, suggest acting out a dialogue between Jeroboam and his advisors about the people going back to Jerusalem to make sacrificial worship. The biblical passage does not say that Jeroboam had advisors, but he likely did consult with others on this issue. Invite a class member to become Jeroboam and two other class members to become his advisors. Divide the rest of the class in half to serve as coaches for Jeroboam and for his advisors. Coaches can both verbally prompt their actors and hand them written notes with ideas of what to say.
- Again, stop the dialogue when it is going strong. (Remember, the class members feel more successful that way than if you let the dialogue die out with actors not knowing what to do next.)

Dimension 3:
What Does the Bible Mean to Us?

(I) Explore the people's view: To your tents, O Israel!

- Reread 1 Kings 12:16 aloud. This is the storyteller's description of how the people of the northern tribes of Israel felt about Solomon's oppression and how they responded to Rehoboam's promise to make it even harder on them.
- Invite class members to identify current situations in the world where a population of people are experiencing oppression. After they have identified several situations, ask them to work in pairs to rewrite verse 16 (the poetic part) in today's words as if it came from one of the modern oppressed groups. Suggest that they try their hands at a poetic version to fit the modern situation.
- Invite pairs to share their prose and poetic efforts and to reflect on any insights they got into the current situations in the world.
- Possible discussion questions:
  1. How is the current situation like the one described in Kings? How is it different?
  2. How does the current situation look and feel from the point of view of the people who are oppressed?

(J) Write about change.

- Invite class members to write their ideas about the topic: "How I feel about changes that are made in our church's worship practices."
- If some do not like to write, offer them clay or paper and paints or colored markers. Suggest that they express their feelings about changes in worship practices in symbolic form. Encourage them to select colors, shapes, and symbols to express feelings about changes in worship.
- When class members have finished, invite both groups back together. Invite one or two to share if they wish, but do not push.
- Focus a brief discussion on class members' feelings about changes in general. Do they like change? Why, or why not? What helps them to accept changes in something that has been familiar? What hinders them?

(K) List the pros and cons of religious purity.

- Divide class members into two teams, giving each team several sheets of newsprint and markers.
- Ask one team to list all the advantages or "pros" for maintaining a strict obedience to old ways of worship that are more biblical or pure.
- Ask the other team to list all the disadvantages or "cons" to maintaining old ways that are more biblical or pure.
- When both teams have finished, have the teams exchange their lists. Each team is now to study the other team's list and identify the truths and advantages in that team's list. Give them time to struggle with this. Having just composed advantages for one view, it will take a little time for teams to see advantages in a totally opposite view. Keep gently urging team members to get below the surface and find the real truths in the other team's statements.
- Bring the groups together (and suggest that they mix their seating so they are no longer seated as "teams"). Then invite class members to reflect on the advantages and disadvantages of maintaining purity in worship practices today.

(L) Discuss the images of oppressor/liberator kings.

- Review the main points of the last section of Dimension 3 in the study book (page 28) with the class members. When they have in mind the notions of Rehoboam and Jeroboam as oppressor and liberator, ask these questions:
  1. Bible scholar Richard Nelson says that some Christians today who provide religious legitimacy for the status quo should remember the first part of the story about Rehoboam and Jeroboam. What does he mean?

2. Nelson also says that other Christians who offer the church's blessing on all liberation movements should remember the last part of the story of Rehoboam and Jeroboam. What is he saying about those Christians?
3. Which part of Nelson's comments is hardest for you to understand? (Sometimes we understand what our "enemy" should do better than we understand what we should do. Whichever question was hardest to understand might well be something your class members should struggle with some more!)

(M) Take another look at a hard question about God.

- Invite class members to examine again the biblical idea that God guides history.
- Possible questions to explore:
  1. To what extent do you think that God caused the downfall of Solomon's monarchy?
  2. To what extent did God engineer the conflict between Rehoboam and Jeroboam?
  3. To what extent did God cause Rehoboam to choose the wrong advisors?
  4. To what extent did God influence Jeroboam to make those worship reforms that later the storyteller of Kings would condemn?
  5. How do you think God interacts with human events in ordinary history?
- After discussing some of these questions, remind class members that this issue is one we will keep revisiting throughout this unit. Urge them to keep thinking about it and to keep their minds open for further insights.

Additional Bible Helps

Israelite Worship: Visions, Practices, and Reforms
The Hebrew word that we translate as "worship," says *Harper's Bible Dictionary*, meant "'to bow down, prostrate oneself,' a posture indicating reverence and homage given to a lord, whether human or divine" (page 1143). Worship was modeled after the service given to human sovereigns. The sovereign lived in a palace with servants who offered food; washed, anointed, and clothed him; scented the air with incenses; lit lamps at night; and guarded the doors to the palace. The deity lived in a temple where priests made sacrifices of food; washed, anointed, and clothed it; scented the air with incense; guarded the doors of the temple; said prayers; and bowed down. The deity was worshiped as a human sovereign might be worshiped (page 1143). Although the *Harper's Bible Dictionary* says "this was especially prominent in pagan religions," the description above sounds very much like Old Testament worship of the LORD.

The *Harper's Bible Dictionary* also notes that "although Israelite worship shared many of these external forms, . . . its essence was quite different" (page 1143). The traditional, long-accepted distinction between paganism and Israel's religion was that for the Israelites, worship of God meant not only external worship rituals but more importantly obedience to the moral and ethical laws of God. Sacrifices and other rituals were performed to honor God. Moreover, it was of utmost importance *who* was being worshiped.

The ideal worship for Israelites is described in various instructions in the books of Exodus, Leviticus, and Numbers. These instructions were written by a group of writers called "Priestly writers" by scholars. The most prominent feature of Israelite worship is sacrifice, a gift to God. These Priestly books were written in the sixth century B.C. (500's) during the Exile. Some speculate that these priestly instructions on worship were written by priests who were anticipating the return of the Israelite people to their lands.

Sacrificial offerings were of several kinds. The burnt offering was the most common and probably the oldest form of sacrifice and used for atonement or thanksgiving purposes to win the favor of the LORD. Other types of offerings included the peace offering, thank offering, freewill offering, votive offering, ordination offering for the high priest, sin offering (really a purification ritual to cleanse the sanctuary of impurity), guilt offering, and cereal offering. (See *Harper's Bible Dictionary*, "Worship" for more details.)

People participating in worship needed to be ritually clean. Being unclean was not a crime, though it kept the person from worship. It only became a crime if, after the period of impurity, the person did not follow the proper cleansing rituals.

Information about offerings and about ritual and cleanliness instructions are offered in great detail by the Priestly writers in Exodus, Leviticus, and Numbers.

In the Book of Deuteronomy we read of slightly different versions of worship rituals. The Deuteronomist insisted on a single central sanctuary for sacrifices, which led to many "profane" sacrifices since Jerusalem was too far away for many worshipers.

Those are the ideal images: the Priestly version and the Deuteronomist's version. In reality, however, the Israelite people practiced their worship much differently. Early patriarchs like Abraham and Jacob offered sacrifices at temporary altars, serving as their own "priests." During the time of the judges, priests and temples became known; but the earlier practices continued. During Solomon's time, even after the Temple was built in Jerusalem, people continued to offer sacrifices at local outdoor altars.

In summary, the worship of the Israelites was under constant change, never quite measuring up to the ideal versions lifted up by the Priestly writers or the Deuteronomist.

Seen in this larger context of Israelite worship practices, the reforms of Jeroboam do not seem so terrible. He was trying to make worship accessible to the people in a new situation. The two golden calves that Jeroboam ordered made possibly were intended to replicate the oxen that were part of Solomon's Temple in Jerusalem (1 Kings 7:25; 12:28). Nonetheless, the Deuteronomist condemns them as idolatrous.

Why then does the Deuteronomist react so negatively? Probably because in his day during the Exile it was important to rally the exiled and demoralized peoples around older practices and visions that would help them reclaim their identity as God's people.

The United and Divided Monarchy

The Israelite monarchy was begun by King Saul, following the period of the judges. The monarchy was firmly established by David and greatly enhanced by Solomon. The united monarchy, with one king, lasted one hundred years (approximately 1020 B.C. with the beginning of Saul's reign to 922 B.C. at the end of Solomon's reign).

When the monarchy divided, it became the Northern Kingdom of Israel and the Southern Kingdom of Judah. The Northern Kingdom of Israel consisted of ten ancient northern tribes of Israel. The Southern Kingdom consisted of two tribes: Judah and Benjamin. Each kingdom of the divided monarchy had its own king and its own capital (Jerusalem in the south; Shechem and then Tirzah in the north). The divided monarchy lasted two hundred years, from 922 to 721 B.C. when Samaria was conquered by the Assyrians and the Northern Kingdom of Israel fell.

The Southern Kingdom of Judah lasted another one hundred thirty-five years, until Jerusalem fell to the Babylonian invasion in 587/586 B.C.

4 "My God Is Greater Than Yours!"

1 Kings 11:1-7;
18:17–19:3
2 Kings
21:1-19

LEARNING MENU

Keeping in mind the ways your class members learn best, as well as their needs and interests, choose at least one learning segment from each of the three Dimensions.

Dimension 1: What Does the Bible Say?

(A) Map activity.

- You will need a Bible dictionary, construction paper for arrows, scissors, pins, and a felt-tipped marker to add items to the wall map of the divided monarchy. If you have not used the wall map before, hang one for this session and invite class members to add items from previous sessions. (See activity "A" in chapters 1, 2, and 3.)
- Ask class members to find and mark the following places with arrows:
—Mount Carmel (This is a mountain range. It is not near the city of Carmel.);
—The city of Sidon (Jezebel's home) in Phoenicia;
—Samaria and Jezreel (the two capitals of Ahab's reign).

(B) Add to wall timeline.

- You will need a Bible dictionary and whatever art materials are needed to add to the wall timeline.
- Ask class members to look up dates and add King Ahab and Queen Jezebel to the wall timeline. Read about Ahab and Jezebel in the Bible dictionary.
- Ask students to prepare a short report on two views of Jezebel.

(C) Find out more about Baal and Asherah.

- You will need a Bible dictionary and a commentary or two that include First Kings. (See the "Suggested Resource List," page 71, for suggestions.)
- Ask class members to research the following questions and prepare a short report:
  1. What does the Bible say about Asherah and Baal?
  2. What do various biblical scholars say about Asherah and Baal in Bible dictionaries and commentaries?
  3. What appears to be the Bible's stance regarding pagan religion?

(D) Explore the Israelite land law.

- Ask persons to reread 1 Kings 21:1-3. Then look up

Leviticus 25 to discover what Israel's basic assumption about land is.
- Clue: If students are having trouble finding the basic assumption in the midst of verses about specific use of the land, suggest they look at verses 1, 2, and 23 in Leviticus 25.

> **THE ISRAELITE LAND LAW**
> **Leviticus 25:1-2; 23-24**
>
> Leviticus 25 lays out the basic assumption about land for the Israelite people. First and foremost, the land belongs to the LORD God. It is a gift from God to the people: "When you enter the land that I am giving you . . ." (Leviticus 25:2). The same assumption is clearly present in 25:23: "The land shall not be sold in perpetuity, for the land is mine [God's]; with me [God] you [the Israelite people] are but aliens and tenants. . . ." Chapter 25 also describes various specific laws governing use and care of the land and redemption of land that has changed hands.

(E) Review study book questions and hear reports.

- If some persons have not read the study book materials and completed the questions in Dimension 1, give them time to do so. Other students may work on activities "A," "B," "C," or "D."
- Quickly review answers to the questions before moving on to activities in Dimensions 2 and 3.
- Suggested answers:
  1. Solomon's sin is his love of foreign wives and his turning toward their religion and away from worship of the LORD. (See 1 Kings 11:1-13.) Ahab also commits this sin by marrying Jezebel from Sidon and supporting her worship of Baal and Asherah.
     Note: While discussing this question have those who did the map activity point out where Sidon is.
  2. The basic contest between Baal and the LORD involves the setting up of altars to each with dry wood. The greater god will be able to light the wood. In addition, the greater god will bring rain to end the drought.
  3. Jezebel is furious when she hears that Elijah was successful with his contest and that he had all her prophets of Baal and Asherah seized and killed. She threatens to kill Elijah within a day.
     Note: While discussing this question, have those who did the map activity point out where Mount Carmel is.
  4. Ahab cannot have Naboth's vineyard because it is part of Naboth's "ancestral inheritance." It belongs to his family; and according to Israelite land laws, he is not supposed to sell it or trade it away forever, which is what the king wanted (1 Kings 21:3; Leviticus 25:23).

Note: While discussing this question, have those who did the map activity point out where Naboth's home, Jezreel, is.

Dimension 2: What Does the Bible Mean?

(F) Discuss hard questions.

- Discuss these questions:
  1. According to the storyteller of Kings, what is God's guidance to the Israelites about foreign wives? Why? (See background article, "Foreign Wives/Foreign Faith," on page 21, and Deuteronomy 7:3-4; 13:6-11; 17:17a.)
  2. Is there more than one way to look at Jezebel's role in the two stories about Elijah? What are the different views?
  3. Who is the real troubler of Israel (1 Kings 18:17-18)? Is it Elijah? Ahab? Jezebel? the storyteller of Kings? The LORD God? Why, or why not? What case might be made for each of these persons being a troubler in some ways?
  4. Is Elijah's boast that "my god is greater" a reasonable boast? What fear lay behind Elijah's boast? How did his boast and contest contribute to the storyteller's message? How did it affect the Israelite people in their ongoing struggles to live in the midst of other people who had different faiths?
  5. Kings and queens have power over their people and the land. How does this concept of "power over" sometimes get corrupted? Who is using power in a corrupt way in our biblical stories in today's lesson— Solomon? Ahab? Elijah? Jezebel? Why and how is their use of power corrupt?

(G) Examine the role of prophets with the Israelite kings and monarchy.

- Say to class members: "The Pledge of Allegiance states that we are 'one nation under God. . . .' Our coins have the motto: 'In God We Trust.' Yet the founding fathers of the United States constructed a government very different from the monarchy of Israel."
- Questions to discuss:
  1. What are the differences you see between our country's government and ancient Israel's?
  2. How are the ways the kings were chosen and our presidents are selected different?
  3. What about the influence prophets and priests had on kings and the influence religious leaders and ministers have on presidents today?
  4. What are differences in the laws?
  5. What are differences in the ways people are treated?

(H) Create three imaginary dialogues.

- You will need newsprint and markers. Make a copy of each scenario below to give to the teams (one scenario per team).
- Divide the class members into three teams. Give each team one of the scenarios below, and ask the teams to create an imaginary dialogue. First each team should talk together about what the dialogue might include. Then two members of the team should actually carry out the dialogue in character.
- —Scenario I: Imagine Jezebel, a princess of Sidon who is being married off to the foreign king Ahab next week, talking with her mother about her upcoming marriage and her move to the "foreign" land of Israel.
- —Scenario II: Imagine Ahab talking with an advisor about his new foreign wife Jezebel and her desire to continue to worship her own gods Baal and Asherah.

  Note: The Bible does not mention an advisor, but Ahab surely had some. Give the advisor a name, feelings, and a point of view about this issue. Ahab is usually described as weak and ineffectual; try playing him another way. What other motives might he have had (besides just being weak and ineffectual) for allowing Jezebel her gods?
- —Scenario III: Imagine Naboth going home to his wife after he has told King Ahab that he will not sell or trade his vineyard to the king. The wife is not mentioned in the Bible. Give her a name and consider what her concerns and feelings might be about this event.
- After the three teams have carried out their dialogues in their teams, call them back together and discuss learnings, insights, questions, concerns they have about the biblical stories.
- If your class is small, assign each of these scenarios to two people. If necessary have two teams working on Scenario II. Have each team of two talk to each other about what should go into their scenario. Then invite each team to do the dialogue for the rest of the class.

Dimension 3:
What Does the Bible Mean to Us?

(I) Study a song line about God's power.

> "This is my Father's world.
> O let me ne'er forget
> that though the wrong seems oft so strong,
> God is the ruler yet."

(First part of stanza 3 of "This Is My Father's World," words by Maltbie D. Babcock; No. 144 in *The United Methodist Hymnal*.)

- Sing this stanza together. Then explore the idea of God as ruler of the world and of history. What do you think this idea would have meant to the exiled listeners of the storyteller of Kings? What does this song phrase mean to you today? Is your idea different from those Israelites long ago? How? Why?

(J) Discuss ideas in the study book.

- As a whole class discuss the following questions:
  1. What do you think about the "exclusive" stance—that the LORD must be worshiped exclusively—projected in the stories in Kings so far?
  2. What do you think about the so-called "pagan religion" mentioned in the Bible? Does the Bible give an accurate view of the old pagan religion? Do you think anyone who totally rejects your beliefs can describe you accurately?
  3. How do we maintain the distinctiveness of our own faith while affirming others' rights to a different view and a different faith? To what extent should we do so?

(K) Explore the religious exclusiveness/diversity struggle today.

- Ask class members to divide into two teams. Provide each team with newsprint and felt-tipped markers.
- One team is to make a list of points to support the position: "Diversity of religions and faiths is good for our country and no threat to my personal Christian faith."
- The other team is to make a list of points to support the position: "The Christian religion is the best religion and should be the official religion of our country; treating all religions equally threatens my personal Christian faith."
- Once the lists are made, invite class members to group themselves in "wise religious leader" and "wise national leader teams" (see Activity "K" in Chapter 1). Hang the two lists so both teams can see them. Ask these wise leader teams to discuss how their wise leader would talk about this issue.
- After they have had time to work on a strategy, invite each team to select a wise leader to represent them. (This should be a different person than the one who did the dialogue for Chapter 1, if Activity "K" was done at that time.)
- Invite the two "wise leaders" to engage in a dialogue about diversity of religions in our country and how Christians might respond to that diversity.

(L) Reflect about personal power.

- Invite class members to write about any incidents in their own lives where they were in a position of power over another person. Copy the following questions on

newsprint so people can refer to them as they are writing.
- Points to reflect on:
—How did you use your power?
—Did you act like Jezebel, wielding your power ruthlessly to accomplish some goal?
—Did you use your power in a "power with" rather than "power over" kind of way?
—How would you use your power differently if you could relive that incident in your life?
- Invite persons who wish to do so to share from their written reflections.

(M) Write a modern story about power.

- Invite class members as individuals or in pairs to create a modern story that is similar to Naboth and his vineyard.
- Questions to consider in choosing the modern episode:
  1. What kind of situation could happen today?
  2. Who would be like Naboth, King Ahab, Jezebel, the elders/nobles, the scoundrels?
  3. Who would have the power? How might they misuse it?
- Invite several people to share the stories they have written.

Additional Bible Helps

Foreign Wives/Foreign Faith

Solomon married the daughter of Pharaoh soon after Solomon became king of Israel. During his long reign he accumulated many more wives and princesses. Many of his marriages were the result of peace and trade treaties with nations and sovereign city-states surrounding Israel.

Given the patriarchal organization of their societies, the fathers of foreign wives probably made the decisions to marry their daughters off to the Israelite king. The women likely had little say in the matter. They were forced to leave their homes, their mothers, their siblings. What would they take with them? their fine clothes, their jewels, some of their servants, and their own faith! Can we blame them?

The women who became the wives of Israel's kings were "foreigners" and "strangers." They did not worship the LORD. They had their own faith. Some worshiped a goddess, who had a young male consort. Many were royal princesses in their own lands and may have served as high priestesses of their religion, or at least as royal supporters.

As they moved from their homes into the foreign land of Israel, the wives continued to practice their faith. However, they did not "bring into Israel the worship of the goddess." The worship of the goddess was already there when the Hebrew people took over the land of Canaan. Evidence suggests that in the early days of the judges a fair amount of intermarrying and mixing of pagan religious customs with the worship of the LORD occurred.

The idea of one male god as the supreme true God came later. Some speculate that the monotheistic worship of the LORD came only during the Exile, with the strong, repeated claims of the Deuteronomistic storyteller and other religious leaders that the LORD insisted on being worshiped exclusively.

The religious leaders in the exilic and postexilic communities knew that to stop a particular practice, they must be very rigid in policing the people and in deploring the pagan religion. Israel's leaders had come to know the Divine One as more universal than many of the popular local understandings of gods and goddesses in their day. They offered the people a "bigger" concept of the Divine than many had had. God was not a local deity who ruled the seas, another local deity who ruled the harvests, and another deity who controlled the rain. Israel's God ruled all of nature and controlled all of history.

With this magnificent idea of the divine available, why were the kings and people of Israel so attracted to the foreign wives' faith? Perhaps because the pagan worship of the goddess and god was tied to the seasons, cycles, and realities of the land and the people. Why did the people and the kings of Israel not fully embrace the concept of a monotheistic god? Perhaps because the worship of the LORD got too abstract and transcendent? Perhaps because the LORD came to be quite sexless? Perhaps because the LORD was too warlike? Perhaps because the LORD was said to be an angry punisher? We do not know for sure.

We do know, however, that over time this wonderful new theological concept of a universal divinity who guides nature and history solidified.

We do not really know all the details of the struggle between pagan religions and Israel's religion in the centuries before the birth of Jesus. Too much of the history has been lost. We only know that the LORD's prophets and priests tried over many centuries to eradicate the worship of gods and goddesses who were related to the fertility of the land and the sexuality of the people. In Ezra-Nehemiah, four hundred years after Solomon died, Israel's leaders are still struggling with "foreign gods."

SAMPLE TIMELINE FOR SESSIONS 1 THROUGH 4

If you have chosen to do Learning Activity "B" during each class session so far, your class members have been developing a timeline with dates for key events. The appearance of your timeline makes no difference; the sample one below happens to move vertically. However, you may wish to check the dates in the sample timeline. They represent consensus opinions among today's biblical scholars.

All the dates on this timeline are "B.C." or "Before Christ." Keep in mind that the numbering of years before Christ runs backwards. The year 1000 B.C. is earlier than the year 950 B.C.

The abbreviation *c.* in front of a date stands for the Latin word *circa*, which means "approximately."

Date	Event	Session
c. 2100	Abraham and Sarah leave Ur	
c. 1700	Joseph arrives as a slave in Egypt	
c. 1250	Moses/Miriam lead Exodus out of Egypt	
c. 1200–1020	Judges lead the people of Israel	Session 1 Learning Activity "B"
c. 1050–1020	Samuel is a prophet who assumes national leadership	
c. 1020–1000	Saul reigns as first king of Israel	
1000–961	David becomes king	
c. 961–928	Solomon builds the Temple	Session 2 Learning Activity "B"
928	End of Solomon's reign	
922–915	Rehoboam's reign over Judah	Session 3 Learning Activity "B"
922–901	Jeroboam's reign over Israel	
869–850	King Ahab and Queen Jezebel	Session 4 Learning Activity "B"

Any Hope in Exile?

LEARNING MENU

Keeping in mind the ways your class members learn best, as well as their needs and interests, choose at least one learning segment from each of the three Dimensions.

Dimension 1: What Does the Bible Say?

(A) Add to the wall map.

- You will need another map, one that shows the larger Middle East area and the Assyrian Empire. The map, "The Assyrian Empire," in *Bible Teacher Kit* (Abingdon, 1994; available from Cokesbury) is a good one; or find a large wall map in your Sunday school files. If you have room, leave up the map of the divided monarchy with the items class members have added. Gather two new colors of yarn, some pins, construction paper, scissors, and a felt-tip marker. You will also need a modern map showing the Middle East today. This does not need to be a large wall map. Again, there is a small map of today's Middle East in *Bible Teacher Kit*, or look for a *National Geographic* map or one at your library. A good Bible dictionary with maps, such as *Harper's Bible Dictionary*, might be useful as persons investigate the Assyrian and Babylonian empires.

  Note: If you cannot find a wall map of the Assyrian Empire, continue to use the map you have of the monarchy and ask students to use a new color of yarn to show the boundaries of Assyria (see the map on the inside back cover of the study book). They can extend the yarn out onto the wall to show the breadth of that empire.

- As class members arrive, ask them to mark the map with one color of yarn to show the boundaries of the Assyrian Empire, including the Northern Kingdom of Israel, but not Judah. Locate on the map and mark with arrows the places where people were deported. See 2 Kings 17:6. Then with the second new color of yarn mark the Babylonian Empire that invaded Judah. Use construction paper arrows to identify the boundary lines of the Assyrian and Babylonian empires.

(B) Add to the wall timeline.

- You will need Bible dictionaries, study books, and the chronology chart on page 72 of this leader's guide for persons to search out dates.
- Add to the wall timeline the following names and events, with their dates:

—Assyrian invasion
—Fall of Samaria
—Josiah's reign
—Huldah the prophetess
—Fall of Jerusalem

(C) Learn about the Assyrian and Babylonian empires.

- Refer students to maps, the chronology chart (page 72 in this leader's guide), Bible dictionaries, several commentaries on Kings, and the article "The Conquerors of Israel and Judah" (page 26).
- Ask them to search out these basic facts on the Assyrian and Babylonian empires:
—When did each come into power?
—When and how did they impact Israel and Judah?
—How long did the empires last?
- Ask persons to prepare a short report to share with the whole class.

(D) Learn about Huldah the prophetess.

- For this activity you will need to have several Bible dictionaries, at least one commentary on Kings, any resources on Old Testament women, and the article "The Prophetess Huldah" (page 27). Suggest that they reread 2 Kings 22:11-20. They should also look up the parallel account in 2 Chronicles 34:22-28.
- Ask students to study materials about Huldah and to prepare a short report.
- Questions to search out:
  1. Who was Huldah? Where did she live?
  2. How many women prophets does the Hebrew Scripture describe?
  3. Why would Josiah seek out Huldah instead of Jeremiah or Zephaniah, who were much more prominent prophets of the same period?
  4. What thoughts do you have about what she said to King Josiah?

(E) Review questions and hear reports.

- Provide time for class members to finish answering the questions in the study book if any need this time. Offer activities "A," "B," "C," and "D" to other students.
- Review the answers to questions quickly and ask for any reports to be given.
- Suggested answers:
  1. Assyrian king Shalmaneser invaded Israel when Israel's king Hoshea stopped paying tribute money to Assyria and instead was sending messengers to the Egyptian king (probably to secure Egypt's aid against Assyria). The storyteller explains further that the Assyrian invasion happened because "the people of Israel had sinned against the LORD their God." The people had worshiped other gods and had neglected to follow God's commandments.
  2. When King Josiah "heard the words of the book of the law, he tore his clothes" (a sign of sorrow and repentance). He then sent his priest and others to "inquire of the LORD" what he should do now that the words of the law had been returned to him and to the people of Judah.
  3. The LORD tells Josiah that, because Josiah has humbled himself before God, Josiah will be spared from "all the disaster that I [the LORD] will bring on this place."
  4. Huldah speaks the word of the LORD to Josiah's priest and servants who come to inquire of the LORD for the meaning of the books of the law found in the Temple.
  5. After twenty-seven years in exile in Babylon, Jehoiachin is released from prison by the Babylonian king and given a seat of honor "in the king's presence."

Dimension 2: What Does the Bible Mean?

(F) Discuss some meanings of the Book of Kings.

- Questions to get started:
  1. How would you describe what God's role is in this lesson's passages from Second Kings, at least according to the storyteller's point of view? (Possible ideas: God is in charge of history and politics and nature. God seems bound in God's own system of punishment and has to punish Josiah even though Josiah institutes religious reforms.)
  2. Is it possible that the storyteller was wrong about who God is and how God interacts with people, history, politics, and nature? Why, or why not?
  3. The issue of purity or syncretism (see glossary, page 111 in the study book) of religion is one of the major issues throughout the Book of Kings. We have looked at this issue in several ways. Now that we are at the end of our study of Kings, what do you think about the storyteller's insistence that God is to be worshiped only in certain ways and that nothing about the pagan religion is good?
  4. The storyteller of Kings has portrayed the LORD as the instigator of some political wars. Assyria and Babylonia invade and destroy the northern and southern kingdoms because this is God's will. Does this mean the Bible favors war or that war is sometimes divinely ordered?

(G) Do a guided visualization of Josiah and the book of law.

- Before class time, find a large picture of Josiah and the law book. If possible find one with Huldah, Shaphan, and Hilkiah in it too. Or use several large pictures. Check in old teaching picture files of children's Sunday school materials.
- In class: Invite students to get comfortable and seated so that they can easily see the large pictures, if you have them. Use the following as a guided visualization, pausing wherever there is a series of dots so students can think and feel.

Take a deep breath in and slowly release it . . . and another. . . . and another. . . . Now imagine that you are one of the servants in King Josiah's palace. . . . You were present when King Josiah sent Shaphan to the Temple where repairs were being carried out. You heard Josiah tell Shaphan, "Go and find the high priest Hilkiah and have him count the money that has been collected from the people. Tell Hilkiah to give the money to the people who are working on the Temple. Tell Hilkiah that he does not have to ask for any accounting from the workers for they are honest people." . . . That was not unusual, but what happened next certainly was. . . . Shaphan came running back to the king, with Hilkiah right behind him. . . . Shaphan is saying that Hilkiah had found the scroll of the law in the Temple. . . . Did he find it in the rubbish, you wonder? . . . Shaphan is reading the book to King Josiah. . . . "These are the statutes and ordinances that you must diligently observe in the land that the LORD, the God of your ancestors, has given you. . . . You must demolish completely all the places where the nations serve their gods. . . . You shall not worship the LORD your God in such ways." . . . There was much more . . . and now the king is tearing his clothes in an act of mourning and grief. Listen, the king is giving another order: "Hilkiah, Shaphan, Ahikam, Asaiah, I want all of you to go to the prophetess Huldah. Ask her what God's word is for us; . . . for these words you have read to me tell me that God's wrath is great against us because our ancestors did not obey God's way. . . ."

You wonder what Huldah will say. . . . You decide to tag along behind; . . . surely she will have good words for King Josiah, for he is already repairing the Temple and doing away with some of the practices of the religion of the goddess. . . . Here she is, the prophetess Huldah; . . . she is listening to Hilkiah and Shaphan. . . . Now she starts to speak: "Thus says the LORD, I will indeed bring disaster on this place and on its inhabitants because they have abandoned me and have made offerings to other gods. I am angry." . . . But now Huldah is saying more: "The LORD also says that because the king's heart is penitent and because he has mourned and grieved, he shall not see all the desolation that God will bring upon the people and the land." . . .

Now you are walking back to the palace slowly, wondering about all the things you heard and saw. . . . What is going to happen to you and the rest of the people and when? . . . Can no one make the LORD change his mind? . . . . . .

When you are ready, return to the present and rejoin the class.

- Ask class members to reflect on this visualization exercise:
—How did you feel being one of the servants in the palace?
—What did you think about what was happening?
—How did you feel about Huldah's messages?
—As a servant, a common person, what was your biggest concern walking back to the palace after hearing Huldah?

(H) Do a dramatic reading of the story of Josiah and the law book.

- You will need five copies of 2 Kings 22 (from the same translation). On one copy highlight the words that Josiah says; on the second copy highlight Hilkiah's words; on the third, Shaphan's words; on the fourth, Huldah's words; on the fifth copy mark all the lines that the narrator will read.
- As class members arrive, invite five people to prepare to do a dramatic reading later in the class time. Suggest that they go off in a corner and practice.
- Invite the dramatic reading team to share the reading. When they have finished, ask the readers first to reflect on any insights they got about their character and about the whole event. Then ask the rest of the class members to reflect on the meaning of the reading.

(I) Write a prayer on the Exile.

- Invite students to write a prayer as if they were one of the people going into Exile from Samaria or Jerusalem or perhaps as one of the people left on the conquered land. Review 2 Kings 17:5-6, 24; and 24:8-12.
- After they have had time to work on their prayers, invite two or three class members to read theirs to the class. Talk about how the invasions must have felt to the common people of Israel.

(J) Write a new stanza to the hymn "Let My People Seek Their Freedom."

"Let My People Seek Their Freedom" (No. 586 in *The United Methodist Hymnal*) is based on Deuteronomy 8:14-18, in which the storyteller's voice reminds us:

Remember it is God who brought you out of slavery in Egypt and provided manna and then prosperity and wealth. Do not think you gained it yourself.

The first stanza is about the Exodus from Egypt; the second one is about Jesus sending disciples to all the nations. In between a whole lot of history has been left out!

- Ask class members to write a new stanza (or maybe two?) to summarize their understanding of the years of the monarchy. Here is one possible way to start such a stanza:

    When God's people lived in Israel
    All the kings had foreign wives

- When the new stanza is written, ask class members to print it in large letters on newsprint (to save for future use). It may be sung at the end of session today and again in later sessions.

Dimension 3:
What Does the Bible Mean to Us?

(K) Discussion Questions

- Discuss these questions:
  1. Explore the experience of being an exiled people today—who are today's exiles in other countries? in our own country? in our churches?
  2. Who are the Huldahs in our religious communities today? What kinds of messages are they sharing from God? How are they treated?
  3. To what extent does the Book of Kings portray the God of Kings in the same way as we understand the God whom we worship today?
  4. To what extent should the exiled people blame themselves and their ancestors for lack of faith?
  5. What do you think about all the political/economic power issues and the greed for land that apparently led to the invasions and the fall of a small monarchy? To what extent do you believe that God directs oppressors to crush people and nations? Was God directing these wars?
  6. Is the image of God presented in Kings big enough for us in our century?
  7. How do you understand the storyteller's whole story of the kings of Israel?

(L) Write about a personal experience of exile.

This activity would be a good follow-up to activity "I."

- Suggest that class members think about a time or event where they felt like they personally were "in exile." Suggest that they write a personal prayer about exile or a reflection statement about their experience of being in exile today.
- After participants have had time to work on their prayers and reflections, invite several class members to read their prayers or their written reflections to the whole class.
- If persons seem interested, continue a discussion of how they sometimes experience "being in exile" and how they feel about that. What sense do they make religiously of their experiences?

(M) Fingerpaint or create a symbol.

- Offer finger painting and/or other art forms as an alternative way for class members to express in art their feelings of being "exiled" today from "home."
- Display finished artwork. Invite people to comment on their own piece if they wish.

(N) Close the study of Kings with a song.

- Sing together "Let My People Seek Their Freedom," *The United Methodist Hymnal*, No. 586. Sing the stanza or stanzas that class members wrote earlier (see "J") between the hymn's first and second stanzas.

TO PREPARE FOR NEXT SESSION

Activity "H" in the next session requires a person or persons to undertake research in a library before the class meets next time. Read through Activity "H" (page 29) before your class meets for this session (Session 5), in order to decide if you will use it for Session 6. In that case you will want to ask during Session 5 for a volunteer to do the research and report back the following session.

Additional Bible Helps

The Conquerors of Israel and Judah

The Assyrian Empire was one of the major empires in Old Testament times. It occupied what is now northern Iraq around the Upper Tigris River. Its capital was Assur (modern Qala'at Sharqat in Iraq). Assyria had three distinct periods as an empire: the Old Assyrian period, the Middle Assyrian period, and the Neo-Assyrian period. The Neo-Assyrian period, from 911 to 609 B.C., was its greatest period. This last period was also the only time it had direct contact with Israel.

In the first phase of the Neo-Assyrian period, 911–824 B.C., Assyrian kings finally halted attacks by Aramaeans and counterattacked through Syria. King Ahab of Israel was involved in the battle of Qarqar in 853 (1 Kings 22).

Assyria was trying mostly to neutralize external threats to its empire and to gain "booty and vassals" who could be used in their great building projects (a goal that sounds very much like Solomon's efforts a hundred years earlier!).

From 824 to 744 B.C. Assyria was involved in more military activities against the Aramaeans, which benefited Israel (2 Kings 13:5). Mainly, however, Assyria retreated more and more from the region during those eighty years, which allowed Israel and Judah to expand their territories under Jeroboam II (2 Kings 14:23-29) and Uzziah (uh-ZIGH-uh, 2 Chronicles 26).

By 744 B.C. Assyria's troubles decreased again and royal power again became strong. Now they were not satisfied with neutral neighbors who provided them with "tribute" and slaves. Now they wanted permanent conquest. As they conquered an area and made it a vassal state, they deported the native peoples and brought in peoples from other conquered areas, a method that demoralized the people and destroyed their ability to fight back. However, the system was flawed in that it placed so much burden on the conquered people that they periodically fought back.

The Northern Kingdom of Israel was one group that fought. Israel lost and was totally destroyed; all the people were deported into Assyria (2 Kings 17:1-6). The Southern Kingdom of Judah watched what had happened to Israel and obeyed for a while longer. Judah finally joined a revolt against Sennacherib (suh-NAK-uh-rib) in 704–701 B.C. Sennacherib crushed the revolt but still allowed Judah to retain its vassal state status (2 Kings 18:13–20:21).

All these revolts, plus a civil war, finally took their toll on Assyria. After 607, more vassal states openly defied their Assyrian conquerors, among them King Josiah of Judah (2 Kings 21:24–23:34) and Babylonia, which had new leadership, the Chaldean (kal-DEE-uhn) dynasty of the Medes (meedz). The Chaldeans finally conquered the heart of Assyria in 614–612 B.C. The Assyrians fell back to a smaller area and held out until 610–609 when the Chaldeans, helped by King Josiah of Judah, completely conquered it. The Babylonians/Chaldeans took over most of the territory of the Assyrians.

The city of Babylon, capital of the Babylonian Empire was located along the Euphrates River in what is now Iraq. Babylon covered two thousand acres, making it one of the largest Mesopotamian cities. Babylonian history goes as far back as the sixth millennium B.C. Its first great era was under the Amorites in the nineteenth century B.C. The second great era began in the 700's B.C. when the Assyrian kings also ruled as regents of Babylonia. Merodach-baladan II (mi-roh-dak-BAL-uh-duhn), a Chaldean, became king in Babylonia for a decade when the Assyrian king Sargon II could not defeat him. Sargon was finally successful in 709–707 B.C., and the Babylonian king lost all his power but remained alive.

The Chaldean rulers of Babylonia were joined by the Medes of Media to overthrow the Assyrian Empire. When Cyrus the Great overthrew his Medan overlord about 550 B.C., Media became a province of the Persian Empire. Under Cyrus and later kings of Persia, the Jews were allowed to return from exile, events that are recorded in Ezra and Nehemiah. The Book of Esther also mentions the Medes and Persians.

The Prophetess Huldah

Huldah was a prophetess who lived in Jerusalem near the palace. She was the wife of Shallum, who was the keeper of King Josiah's wardrobe. She was consulted by five of Josiah's male officials after discovery of a "scroll of Moses" in the Temple.

Huldah told the officials that Jerusalem would be destroyed because God willed it that way. Huldah added that Josiah himself would die before the destruction of Jerusalem took place. Her prophecy, though negative, pushed the faithful Josiah to even greater religious reforms (2 Kings 22; 2 Chronicles 34).

Why did Josiah go to Huldah instead of Jeremiah? Did he hope Huldah would reverse what the LORD was reported to have said in the law book that had been found? Did he go to her because of her husband's connection? Was she consulted rather than Jeremiah or Zephaniah because her opinion was more respected, or possibly because she was the wife of a minor Temple official and thus the cult prophet there? We do not know. History does not tell us much about Huldah, but she may have been more prominent than history has allowed. The Jewish Mishnah says the two southern gates to the Temple Mount were called the Huldah Gates, which means she must have had some prominence.

The Women's Bible Commentary notes that Huldah's prophecy is different from other prophecies in one way. She responds to a written document, which no other prophets before her had done. King Josiah recognized the book of the law as authentic, but the prophet Huldah was needed "to set its truth in motion." She not only interprets the words of the book that was found but also turns out to have authorized the first document of what will become sacred scripture for Judaism and Christianity.

(The material for the section on Huldah is based on *The Women's Bible Commentary*, edited by Carol A Newsom and Sharon H. Ringe, Westminster/John Knox Press, 1992, page 109; *WomanWisdom*, by Miriam Therese Winter, Crossroad, 1991, pages 335–39; and *Harper's Bible Dictionary*, James L. Mays, general editor, Harper & Row, 1988, "Huldah," page 410.)

6 New Occasions Bring New History

1 Chronicles 9:1–44; 10:1–14; 13:1–14

LEARNING MENU

Keeping in mind the ways your class members learn best, as well as their needs and interests, choose at least one learning segment from each of the three Dimensions. Each Dimension offers activities for discussion and more creative type activities. You might want to consider doing at least one active type activity in this session.

Dimension 1: What Does the Bible Say?

(A) Add to the wall map.

- Hang or rehang a large wall map of the united monarchy. You will also need a Bible dictionary, a sheet of colored construction paper, scissors, and tape or thumb tacks.
- Ask class members to locate Mount Gilboa where Saul's final battle took place. Mark it with a big paper arrow on which *Mount Gilboa* is written. Using a Bible dictionary, look up *Gilboa* to learn more.

(B) Play an outline card game.

- This activity was offered in Chapter 1. If you did not do it then or if only a few persons participated, use it in this session to help students put this Kings-to-Esther study into its larger context. See full details on page 3 (Chapter 1, Activity "A"). You will need to prepare the cards ahead of class time. Activity "C" below is an alternative activity.
- Conclude this activity by pointing out that the class members have studied the end of the primary history (Kings) and now are looking at the secondary history (Chronicles through Esther).

(C) Look at one view of the Old Testament.

- To do this activity, students will need a copy of the background article "Two Histories of Israel," page 68.
- Research questions:
  1. What twelve books of the Bible are included in this description of "the primary history of Israel"?
  2. What five books are included in "the secondary history of Israel"?
  3. Why use these two descriptions rather than the more familiar divisions of Law, Prophets, and Writings?

(D) Add to and review the timeline.

- For this activity you will need a Bible dictionary and a list of items for class members to add to the timeline. (If you did not start a timeline in Chapter 1, this would be a good time to start one. See activity "B" on page 4 for materials you will need to create a timeline. Also look back through Chapters 1–5 at the timeline activity and make a list of major people and events for persons to put on the timeline.)
- Ask class members to add these to the timeline:
  —Saul's reign (1020–1000);
  —The end of the Exile;
  —The Persian Empire (the ruling power of the Mesopotamian area during the return from Exile).
- Then ask them to figure out approximately how many years you are backtracking from the last session to this session. (Clue: In Session 5, Kings ended during the Exile; this session looks at Saul's reign.)

(E) Find out who the Chronicler was.

- You will need a Bible dictionary, one or two Bible commentaries on Chronicles, a copy of the article on page 31, "Who Is the Chronicler?" and a copy of the article "The Audience of the Chronicler Storyteller," page 70. Also refer class members to their study book, first paragraph on page 45.
- Ask early-arriving class members to find out what scholars say about "the Chronicler"—when he wrote and to whom. Ask them to prepare a short report for the whole class before you review the Dimension 1 questions in the study book. They might do their report in the form of an "interview with the Chronicler."
- An alternative way to do this activity is for you, as teacher, to prepare a "mini-lecture." Your mini-lecture should have four points:
  1. Who was the Chronicler?
  2. When was Chronicles written?
  3. What are the major sections of Chronicles?
  4. Who was the first audience?
- Give this mini-lecture before reviewing the Dimension 1 questions in the study book.

(F) Compare the two storytellers.

- Invite some class members to compare the Chronicler's story of how David became king (1 Chronicles 11) with the Deuteronomistic storyteller's earlier version in 2 Samuel 1–5.
- Read both versions and then make three lists on newsprint:
  1. all the things the Chronicler completely omits;
  2. all the things the Chronicler changes in his version of the story; and
  3. any items or details the Chronicler adds that the earlier Deuteronomistic storyteller did not include at all.
- Ask class members to be prepared to share the results of their research with the whole class.

(G) Review Dimension 1 questions in study book.

- If some class members have not answered the questions in Dimension 1, give them time to do so. Others may work in small teams on activities "A" through "F."
- Quickly review answers to the questions before moving on to activities in Dimensions 2 and 3.
- Suggested answers:
  1. David, with the help of Samuel, is given credit for establishing the gatekeepers along with numerous other positions and decisions about the Temple. The Chronicler is adding all these details to establish his case that David, the ideal king, really did most of the planning for the Temple and related positions and customs.
  2. Saul is judged unfaithful by the Chronicler for not keeping "the command of the LORD." The Chronicler does not elaborate on what command Saul did not keep, although he notes that Saul consulted a medium rather than relying on God.
  3. David proposes that the ark of God be moved to Jerusalem. Again, the Chronicler is rearranging and selecting material from the previously known stories of David (in First and Second Samuel) to make a point about David's great concern for religious matters.

Dimension 2: What Does the Bible Mean?

(H) Look at genealogies.

- Share ideas with class members from the box in this leader's guide, "Another Look at Genealogies," page 30.
- Discussion questions to get started:
  1. Why were genealogies important in biblical times? Is the reason any different today?
  2. How do different cultures do genealogies, and why?
  3. What place do women have in various genealogies? Why?
- An alternative way to do this activity is to ask several persons to do library research before class time on lineage patterns in Native American, African, Asian, and Hispanic cultures and to bring in a report. Suggest that they look under *anthropology* for references to kinship patterns. One such book is Robin Fox's *Kinship and*

NEW OCCASIONS BRING NEW HISTORY

Marriage: An Anthropological Perspective (Cambridge University Press, 1984), which explores a variety of cultural kinship patterns that would lead to different kinds of genealogies, including patterns in which lineage is traced through the mother instead of the father.

ANOTHER LOOK AT GENEALOGIES

Biblical genealogies come out of a patriarchal society where people trace the male lineage. Those of us today who are of Euro-American ancestry also use this same form of genealogy. We generally trace our father's family name back through the generations. Even when we decide to trace our mother's lineage, we are using her father's name to trace back the generations. The patriarchal form of genealogy served as legal documentation for several purposes in Old Testament times:

—to establish a kinship pattern for inheritance purposes;
—to establish a person's early tribal ancestry for land ownership, for prestige, and for entry into the Hebrew priesthood (priests had to be from the tribe of Levi);
—to document nobility;
—to trace one's lineage back to someone who received an important ancestral appointment.

Not all people, however, use the patriarchal form of genealogy to trace their kinship ties. Native Americans, for example, trace their family connections very differently. Gary Witherspoon in Volume 10 of the *Handbook of North American Indians* (Smithsonian Institution, 1983; page 524) notes that Navajos have "60 or more matrilineal clans called *dine'e'* or *doon'e*." The mother-child bond is primary and her or his father must be of a different clan than the mother. The child is "born for" her or his father's clan and born "in" or "of" her or his mother's clan. Edmund J. Ladd in Volume 9 of the *Handbook* notes that in Zuni tribes the "mother's household is the social, religious, and economic unit," which is composed of "an older woman, her sisters, and the married and unmarried daughters to which from time to time are added various male relatives and in-laws" (page 482).

Native American matrilineal genealogies, like biblical patriarchal ones, are used to pass on land or, in the case of pueblos, the home; but in this case the inheritance goes to the daughter. Because the Native American custom often is to marry outside one's clan, genealogies are also used to trace back clan connections to be certain one is not marrying someone who is considered part of your clan. The Tony Hillerman novel, *Sacred Clowns* (HarperCollins, 1993), has a subplot where a Native American man and woman are tracing back their clan connections to be certain they would not be violating this custom by getting married.

(I) Outline a new history of God's people.

- Divide the class members into several small groups. Ask each group to assume that they are a modern-day "Chronicler" who is trying to speak to Christians today. Invite each group to create an outline of how they might present Israel's history.
—What can Israel's history teach us today?
—What would be the main point or points they as the modern Chronicler would want to emphasize for today's people and today's churches about the kings and the people of Israel?
—How would a modern Chronicler evaluate the kings? the foreign wives? the innovations in worship?
- Encourage the groups just to get the major ideas listed on paper. After they have had time to work, call them together to share their ideas.

Dimension 3: What Does the Bible Mean to Us?

(J) Discuss ideas and meanings about change.

- Using the study book's Dimension 3 as background, discuss the major ideas about change.
- Questions to start with:

1. How do we revise our national history? Why have we revised pieces of our national history? (Here you might explore with the class members how our country has revised, expanded, or changed its understanding of the war in Vietnam over the past few decades. Another example would be how history textbooks were written from the white male point of view and how some history books are now being rewritten to include the Native American and Afro-American sides of historical events as well as more about women's roles in American history.)

2. Why are different ways of doing genealogy relevant to us? (Idea to wrestle with: Does how we trace our lineage show at least part of the power structure in our culture?)

3. What massive world changes have taken place in our lifetime? List these out quickly on a chalkboard, markerboard, or newsprint. Then explore the importance of seeing ourselves as God's people on a journey rather than God's people following an unchangeable pattern of worship or a set of unchanging rules.

4. How does the "gospel" stay the same when the Bible gets interpreted differently by different generations of God's people?

(K) Act out song charades about change.

- Divide the class members into teams of two to four people. Give each team one of the hymn phrases below and ask them to decide how they will act out the phrase as a charade.
- Hymn phrases:
  a. "New occasions teach new duties, Time makes ancient good uncouth [strange or awkward]" ("Once to Every Man and Nation," *The Methodist Hymnal*; The United Methodist Publishing House, 1966; No. 242).
  b. "This is a day of new beginnings, time to remember and move on" ("This Is a Day of New Beginnings," *The United Methodist Hymnal*; The United Methodist Publishing House, 1989; No. 383).
  c. "In the midst of changing ways give us still the grace to praise" ("Many Gifts, One Spirit," *The United Methodist Hymnal*, No. 114, stanza 1).
  d. "As the old ways disappear, let your love cast out our fear" ("Many Gifts, One Spirit," *The United Methodist Hymnal*, No. 114, stanza 2).
  e. "The church of Christ, in every age beset by change but Spirit-led, must claim and test its heritage and keep on rising from the dead" ("The Church of Christ, in Every Age," *The United Methodist Hymnal*, No. 589).

BASIC CHARADE SIGNS

"first word"—hold up one finger

"second word"—hold up two fingers

"sounds like"—pull ear (use this to indicate that the word you are acting out sounds similar to the words you want people to guess; for example, act out *race* to get group to guess *grace*)

"longer version of word guessed"—put hands together and then slowly pull them apart

"shorter version of word guessed"—hold hands apart and then slowly move them together.

- Summarize this activity with a short discussion about the place of change in our faith. Possible questions:
  1. What kinds of changes are we living through today personally? in our church? in our nation? in our world? How do these changes compare with the changes that the Hebrew people went through during and after the Exile?
  2. In the midst of change, biblical history may get revised, biblical passages may get reinterpreted, and biblical "facts" may change with new knowledge. What remains constant in our faith is the "basic gospel message." How do you describe that message?

(L) Reflect on changed interpretations.

- Invite class members to write about an event in their life that they told one way when it happened and that they tell another way today. Suggest that they explore why they have changed their description and interpretation of this event. After allowing time to write, invite two or three students to share general insights into how and why they changed the way they described their personal event. They may or may not want to actually share the event, depending on how personal it is.

(M) Write a litany prayer about faith change.

- You will need several sheets of newsprint and markers. Invite the class members to write lines of thanksgiving for good from the past and lines of hope or praise for the future and its changes. Some lines might also be lines of confession about feelings and attitudes about change.
- As the closing activity for this session sing the litany response, using the two phrases below:
- Sing:
  "This is a day of new beginnings,
  time to remember and move on" [first 2 lines, stanza 1].
- Pray:
  [a line that the class has composed].
- Sing:
  "This is a day of new beginnings;
  our God is making all things new" [last 2 lines, stanza 4].
- Pray:
  [another line the class composed].
- Repeat the pattern until all the class prayer lines have been used. If the class members have composed many lines, group them and read two or three lines in between each sung response.

(Song lines are from "This Is a Day of New Beginnings," *The United Methodist Hymnal*, No. 383.)

Additional Bible Helps

Who Is the Chronicler?

The Chronicler is the name given to the person or persons who wrote First and Second Chronicles, Ezra, and Nehemiah. The Chronicler is thought to have written all four books because they have similar literary features and theological interests. Tradition has long said that this Chronicler was probably a Levite or priest living sometime in the 400's B.C.

Some scholars today think that Ezra and Nehemiah may not have been written by the Chronicler but by an independent writer. These scholars base their decisions on inconsistencies between Ezra-Nehemiah and First and Second Chronicles, such as the lack of importance of King David to Ezra-Nehemiah. Other scholars today still think that Ezra and Nehemiah may have been written by the Chronicler, noting that all the books are focused primarily on the Temple and worship reform and that this is Chronicles' main interest in the monarchy. These scholars believe that in fact Chronicles, Ezra, and parts of Nehemiah may have been all one book originally, with Chronicles telling of the downfall and destruction of the monarchy and Ezra-Nehemiah telling about the return from the Exile. Regardless of whether the books were all written by one writer, they all obviously come from the same religious or literary group.

The Chronicler presents a Secondary History of Israel that is both similar to and different from the Primary History compiled by the Deuteronomistic historians. While both histories begin with creation, the Deuteronomist spends much time with the early years and early people. The Chronicler jumps from a brief list of genealogies right to a description of the monarchy. He skips the garden of Eden, the patriarchs, the whole Exodus event, the stories of the conquest of Canaan by the Hebrew people, and the rule by judges. The Chronicler's major interest is with David and Solomon. Moreover, both of these kings of Israel are important to the Chronicler, not as warriors or builders of the monarchy, but as creators and builders of the Temple in Jerusalem and founders of the worship practices at that Temple. Both David's and Solomon's mistakes and misdemeanors are omitted from the Chronicler's story. The Chronicler's interest in later kings also focuses narrowly on how loyal each king was to the Temple in Jerusalem and on their worship reforms (Hezekiah, Manasseh, Josiah) or failures (Ahaz). The Chronicler's history of Israel thus seems to be primarily a history of the establishment of true worship of the LORD God and the maintenance of that worship at the Temple in Jerusalem.

In contrast the Primary History by the Deuteronomistic historians had a broader concern for the development of the Israelites as "God's people." It was more broadly concerned with the rise of Israel's national life and with its various forms of leadership (warriors, judges, prophets, kings), all of which prove finally to be disastrous for Israel. As David Clines has pointed out, the Primary History of the Deuteronomist is a story of "fair beginnings" in the garden of Eden, in the Exodus, in the arrival in Canaan/Promised Land, in the establishment of the monarchy. And it is a story of "foul endings"—Adam and Eve being kicked out of the garden, slavery in Egypt, punishment after punishment for the people who never quite live up to the LORD's demands until finally the people are sent into Exile (*Harper's Bible Commentary*, pages 75–78).

For the Chronicler punishment by the LORD is not inevitable and complete. Lost wars are judgments from God and victories are evidence of faith. God responds to the faithful and rewards them with success. The Exile is the result of final disloyalty and disregard of prophetic warnings, but hope is definitely present in the list of returned exiles in 1 Chronicles 9 as well as in the final two verses of Second Chronicles.

Some scholars see the Chronicler's voice as a continuation of the Deuteronomist's message, refined with the Chronicler's concern for holiness and purity. Other scholars, like Roddy Braun in his introduction to Chronicles in *Harper's Bible Commentary*, note that "by omission, addition, and alteration . . . [the Chronicler] wrote a new or radically revised picture of Israel's history, which must have been meant to portray more adequately his understanding of Israel's past and of its future hope" (page 342).

Why did the Chronicler write his work? Some scholars have thought his motives were political: to defend the legitimacy of Judah (his community) against the northern community of Samaria. Others have thought his motives were to express hope for the eventual restoration of the Davidic monarchy. Biblical scholar David Clines believes it more likely that his motives were simply to reassure his audience that their lives were valued and that they as a community were indeed carrying out the worship of God "which is the primary function of Israel, indeed, the chief purpose of the world's creation" (*Harper's Bible Commentary*, page 84).

7 TRAGIC MISTAKES AND NEW BEGINNINGS

2 Chronicles 35:16-25; 36:11-21

LEARNING MENU

Keeping in mind the ways your class members learn best, as well as their needs and interests, choose at least one learning segment from each of the three Dimensions. Activities "A," "B," and "C" are set up so that persons can work alone or in small teams as they first arrive in the classroom if you wish. Then you can call them together for the opening prayer, reports, and activity "D." Or you may choose from the Dimensions and build your own session plan.

Dimension 1: What Does the Bible Say?

(A) Add to the wall map.

- You will need a Bible dictionary, a sheet of colored construction paper, scissors, and tape or thumb tacks. Ask class members to locate and mark with large arrows, the sites of the battles that Pharaoh Neco was engaged in: Carchemish on the Euphrates (2 Chronicles 35:20) in Assyria and the plain of Megiddo (2 Chronicles 35:22) in northwestern Palestine. Have them prepare a short report about Megiddo's importance to Judah.

(B) Add to the timeline.

- Ask class members to look up the Egyptian pharaoh Neco in a Bible dictionary and add the dates of his reign to the timeline. If Josiah is not on the timeline, add dates of his reign also. Ask this team to compare the Chronicler's story of Josiah and Neco in 2 Chronicles 35:20-24 with the Deuteronomist's version in 2 Kings 23:29-30. Why would the Chronicler tell the story this way? Clue: The key to the Chronicler's interpretation is that the words of Neco come from God.

(C) Be Bible researchers.

- You will need Bible dictionaries (*Harper's Bible Dictionary* and Volume E–J of *The Interpreter's Dictionary of the Bible* will be especially helpful), commentaries on Chronicles (including *The Women's Bible Commentary* if possible), and copies of the "Additional Bible Helps" at the end of this chapter. Different small teams might research each of the following topics and prepare a short report.
- Research topics:
—Israelite life in Exile (Suggest that this team read Psalm 137 as part of their research.)
—Sabbatical years and the length of Exile
—Women in Chronicles
- Ask teams to share their reports before reviewing the questions in the study book (see next activity).

TRAGIC MISTAKES AND NEW BEGINNINGS 33

(D) Review Dimension 1 questions in study book.

- If some persons have not read the study book and answered the questions in Dimension 1, encourage them to do so while others are working on activities "A," "B," and/or "C."
- Quickly review answers to the questions before moving on to activities in Dimensions 2 and 3.
- Suggested answers:
  1. Josiah commanded that a great Passover Feast be held.
  2. Neco said that Josiah should stop opposing him because Josiah's God ("the LORD") was with Neco.
  3. Josiah did not believe him; he disguised himself to go and fight Neco.
  4. Exile happened as punishment because Israel had ignored God's prophets and because Israel had not properly observed the sabbath.

Dimension 2: What Does the Bible Mean?

(E) Experience the Josiah story.

- Tell the class members that you are going to guide them in a visualization exercise. Read the following italicized words slowly and meditatively. Wherever there is a series of periods, pause to let persons think and feel in silence. Go very slowly!

    Take a minute to get comfortable in your chair. . . . Breathe in and out slowly. . . . Close your eyes if you wish. . . . Let your body relax. . . . Let your mind wander back in time . . . back before the pilgrims landed at Plymouth Rock . . . back before the time of Martin Luther and the Protestant Reformation . . . back before the time of Jesus. . . . Go back five hundred years before Jesus lived. . . . You are one of the people who have recently returned from Exile in Babylonia. . . . Remember how life was for you as a captive in Babylonia. . . . Remember the long tiring walk back to Jerusalem . . . so many weeks to travel. . . . Remember how you felt when you saw Solomon's Temple in ruins. . . . You had heard your grandparents and the priests tell stories of King David and King Solomon and the beautiful Temple so many times, you expected to see it standing there—and then you saw it in ruins. . . . You have been here a few months now, helping clear away the rubble. . . . The leaders are planning to rebuild the Temple. . . . Today you are sitting in the midst of a large crowd who has gathered to hear a new storyteller. . . . He's telling about Israel's past—your past—but he's telling it differently. . . . He's skipped over most of the early stories you have learned about Abraham and Jacob and slavery in Egypt. . . . And even his stories about King David are different somehow.

    Now he is telling about King Josiah and how great he was—almost as great as King David and King Solomon! But what is this? The storyteller is saying that God was speaking through that Egyptian pharaoh Neco! How can this be? God speaking through our old enemy? Yes, that is what the storyteller is saying—that Josiah made a mistake and did not listen when God was trying to tell him something through Neco's voice and that's why Josiah died like he did instead of peacefully as the prophetess Huldah had predicted.

    Now this new storyteller is almost through. . . . He's telling about the destruction of the Temple and the deporting of most of your people. . . . But wait, the end of the story is different; in fact this whole story somehow feels different. . . . He's telling the crowd that we, like Josiah, made a big mistake in not listening to God and not observing proper sabbaths, but that we have paid our debt. The Exile was our punishment, but it is over; now we must go on. . . . God is no longer angry with us and will not continue to punish us for what our ancestors did. . . . If we obey him and worship him properly, prosperity will come to us again.

    Stay in character now, but open your eyes. . . . You are still sitting in the crowd and the storyteller has just finished his new version of your history. How do you feel about his new story? [Pause to let class members answer. Encourage them to stay in character and answer as if they were back in the time of the Chronicler.]

    What was life like for you in Babylonia?

    Did you like the way the storyteller was changing the stories of David and Solomon and Josiah?

    What do you think the storyteller was really trying to say to you with his revised stories?

- To close this experience, say: "The storyteller is finished now with his old, yet new, story. It is time to come back. . . . Slowly bring yourselves forward through the centuries to the present."
- Pause for a few minutes of silence. If you learned the song phrase last week, softly begin singing it: "This is a day of new beginnings." (See activity "M" in Chapter 6, or use hymn No. 383 in *The United Methodist Hymnal*.)

(F) Discuss some questions on meanings.

- Discuss these questions:
  1. What was the Chronicler telling his audience by expanding the story of the "tragic mistake of Josiah"?
  2. What was the overall message of the Chronicler? (Use the box "The Message of the Chronicler" in the study book, page 57, and guide class members to look at the various passages in Chronicles that highlight his message.

3. How does the Chronicler's explanation of the reason for the Exile differ from the explanation of the Deuteronomistic storyteller in Kings?

(G) Illustrate Psalm 137 about Exile experiences.

- Before class, write Psalm 137:1-4 on newsprint, leaving a wide border all around the words. Or if you are allowing enough time, class members could print this out. Invite them to work cooperatively to illustrate these verses with quick sketches using colored markers. While they are working, share ideas from "Additional Bible Helps," "How Did They Feel About the Exile?" (page 37).

> **TEACHING TIP**
> If you have a large class provide more than one sheet of newsprint with the verses printed on it, or hold it until later in the session and give class members a choice between illustrating the verses or making banners (activity "K").

(H) Stage a gentle debate on an issue facing the restoration community.

- Divide the class members into two teams: (a) those who believe the Deuteronomist's explanations of the Exile and (b) the followers of the Chronicler. Have each team choose a spokesperson. (The rest of the team will sit behind or beside that person to "coach.") Pose this question for debate: Which version of the explanation of Israel's experience of exile is "God's word": the Deuteronomist's version or the Chronicler's version?
- Give the teams time to formulate responses within their team. (They will need to have a copy of the "Additional Bible Helps" for this chapter.)
- Then ask spokespersons to make their opening statements. Further responses from each side can be "coached" by team members.

> **TEACHING TIP**
> Give people a little time to get warmed up. If necessary, repeat the debate question a time or two to remind people of their focus. When the debate is going strong, stop it; do not wait for it to falter.

- Conclude this activity by asking the teams to try to collaborate on a statement about God and God's interactions with the Israelite people.
- After the debate examine the experience, using the following questions as starters:
    1. How did you feel about doing this debate? Did it seem relevant to you and your life today? How, or why not?

2. What insights did you gain into the changes that the Jewish people were experiencing after the Exile?
3. What insights did you gain about how the Bible was written and why?

Dimension 3: What Does the Bible Mean to Us?

(I) Examine meanings for us today.

- Engage the class members in a discussion of the three major points in Dimension 3 of their study book.
- Questions to start with:
    1. How do you feel about the idea that God sometimes speaks through our enemies? Have you had experiences of learning some truth from someone you considered an "enemy"?
    2. The Chronicler seems to have gained a less vengeful image of God than the Deuteronomistic storyteller had, which helped him guide the people to move on into the future after the Exile. Like the Chronicler, we usually adjust our image of God when our world, our church, or our personal faith and life situations change and we gain more insight into God's true nature. What is scary about changing our image of God? How does gaining a different image of God sometimes help us?
    3. Refer class members to the "A Pause to Reflect" section in their study book. The Chronicler assumes that God provides prosperity for some because they are faithful and poverty for others because they are unfaithful. Do you agree or disagree with the Chronicler? Is this the kind of image you have of God? Is this your explanation for poverty?

(J) Reflect about prosperity then and now.

- Invite class members to reflect on the Chronicler's assumption that faithfulness to God leads to prosperity and unfaithfulness leads to poverty or destruction of some kind. Questions to reflect on:
—How do you interpret people's prosperity and poverty both back then and now?
—Is God responsible? How?
- Raise the question for the whole class of how we today might reinterpret what happened to the Israelites. How might we today describe God's involvement with them?

(K) Create banners.

- If you are using this activity, decide if each person will create a small banner or if you will suggest that teams of two or three work on a banner. Also decide if you want

class members to create a permanent banner of cloth or a less permanent one of paper. Permanent banners might be hung in the sanctuary.
- You will need appropriate materials: cloth pieces, poster board, or newsprint; paint or markers, or colorful cloth scraps to cut up for words and symbols; yarn, rickrack, or other trimming items.
- Invite individuals or teams to use one or more of the following word pairs to create their banner. They might actually use the words on the banner or they might create symbols for the words:
    exile and return
    repentance and restoration
    faithfulness and prosperity
    unfaithfulness and destruction
    change and constancy
- These words (and others they might choose) reflect the Chronicler's interpretation of history. How class members create the banners will show their own feelings and interpretations of the biblical story of Exile and return.

Additional Bible Helps

Israel's Change of Identity
During the Exile in Babylonia, the basic identity of the people of Judah broke down. They had no land of their own, no capital city, no king to lead them, no political autonomy, no economic prosperity, no strong prophetic leadership and no temple for their worship of God. Consequently, they had to develop a new understanding of themselves, one based less on land, king, and central Temple and more on their new circumstances.

The Jewish people's new identity began to emerge during the Exile and it was strengthened when they returned to the land after the Exile. They learned to live with limited freedom. They were allowed to return "home" but they were still subjects under the rule of a foreign king. Because they were ruled by a governor appointed by the foreign king, they began to look to their priests for leadership. They built a new Temple and concentrated their new identity around it, an identity that is often referred to as "Second Temple Judaism."

The people who returned to the land after the Exile included descendants of both the Northern Kingdom of Israel and the Southern Kingdom of Judah. Northerners and southerners likely were concerned about how to treat one another. Some people from the south probably wanted to sever all ties with the north because the north was seen as particularly sinful. They had seceded from the monarchy and had withdrawn their loyalty from the Jerusalem Temple. However, the Chronicler seems clear that his message is a message to "all Israel," north and south, all who would be loyal to the Jerusalem Temple and its worship practices now that they had returned to the land.

More About the Chronicler?
From the list of the people who returned from Exile in 1 Chronicles 9, we know fairly quickly that the writer of Chronicles lived after the Exile. He is able to name the people who returned to the land. He perhaps lived as early as the mid-to-late sixth century B.C. or as late as the second century B.C. Most scholars use a date of sometime in the fourth century B.C. (late Persian Empire or early Greek Empire).

Women in the Book of Chronicles
The Book of Chronicles differs from the Deuteronomistic history found in Samuel and Kings in many ways. However, its treatment of women is not much different. Women generally are mentioned or omitted in relation to the men who are their fathers, husbands, or sons.

The Chronicler omits women from his revised history of Israel for several reasons. For example, he does not mention several women who were related to David's life because the stories told in Samuel and Kings reflected poorly on David's image as the ideal king in Chronicles. Neither Michal's (MIGH-kuhlz) saving of David from Saul (1 Samuel 19:8-17) nor Abigail's saving of David from shedding Nabal's innocent blood (1 Samuel 25:2-35) is mentioned by the Chronicler, probably because it would not seem "right" for an ideal king to be saved by women. Other stories about women omitted by the Chronicler include: David's adultery with Bathsheba (2 Samuel 11); Amnon's rape of Tamar (2 Samuel 13); Absalom's rape of David's concubines (2 Samuel 16:22); Abishag's presence in David's last days (1 Kings 1:1-4); and Solomon's decision about the two prostitutes (1 Kings 3:16-28).

Careful examination of these passages shows that all of them threaten the Chronicler's portrait of David as Israel's greatest hero. The hero would not take another man's wife or allow the rape of his daughter or his concubines to go unpunished. The Chronicler censors narratives that discredit David. The Chronicler also omits stories of Solomon's extraordinary wisdom. Solomon cannot be greater than David in the Chronicler's mind.

When the Chronicler names a woman in the genealogies, she is presented as the wife of a prominent man who has borne him sons. Occasionally the sister or daughter of an important man is mentioned. Wives and children gave prestige to the faithful man being honored. At least forty-two women are listed in the genealogy; only a few are significant enough to be named elsewhere in the Bible (Keturah, Tamar, Miriam, Bathshua/Bathsheba, and Tamar). Among these forty-some women are the mothers of eleven of the twenty kings of Judah. As queen mothers, these eleven women would be considered the most prominent and respected women in Israel's society.

Other women are omitted by the Chronicler because he omits most of the history of the Northern Kingdom. Thus, Queen Jezebel is omitted because all northern kings are omitted. On the other hand, the Chronicler emphasizes Athaliah (ath-uh-LIGH-uh), mother of King Ahaziah (ay-huh-ZIGH-uh), for her wicked counsel.

One woman enhanced by the Chronicler is Jehoshabeath (jee-huh-SHAB-ee-ath, see 2 Chronicles 22:11 and 2 Kings 11:1-3; Jehosheba [ji-HOSH-uh-buh] in Kings) who saves the young king Joash from Athaliah. The courageous Jehoshabeath is identified as the wife of a priest. One interesting addition made by the Chronicler is found in 2 Chronicles 35:25 where he refers to "all the singing men and singing women" who mourn Josiah's death. This very brief note might (or might not) be a sign that women had a more active part in Temple activities and in the ceremonial moments of Israel than our current version of biblical history leads us to believe. So much of biblical women's history has been lost or never recorded that it is impossible to do more than speculate (adapted from *The Women's Bible Commentary*, pages 110–115).

How Did They Feel About the Exile?

The first audience of the storyteller were greatly scattered and intermixed religiously and ethnically. Their feelings about the Exile were also mixed. From the biblical books of Jeremiah, Lamentations, and Ezekiel we learn that the people during the Exile were depressed and disoriented. Some felt that God was unjust in punishing them for their ancestors' sins (Ezekiel 18:25). Others blamed the prophets for lying and leading them into exile (Lamentations 2:14). The general feeling was: Why pick on us, God? We worship you, unlike those foreign nations. They are the ones you should be punishing, not us! Do not blame us for our ancestors' sins; forgive us for our own sins, and punish our enemies (Psalm 79).

Even those who felt God's punishment was just had lost hope. They were overwhelmed by their losses and homesick for their land and for Jerusalem, the center of their nation and their faith. Those who remained on the land were sometimes smug, believing God still blessed them over the exiled ones. The first audience for the Book of Kings thus was a widely scattered group of people who were all in some way in a state of crisis of faith and the storyteller knew it.

What Does the Storyteller Expect From His Audience?

As he tries to respond to the people's crisis of faith, the storyteller of Kings expects a lot from his audience. He expects them to be literate in the history of the people, knowing Deuteronomy, Joshua, Judges, and Samuel. He expects them to care deeply about the Deuteronomic law. He expects them to have a sense of humor. He expects them to accept literal prophetic predictions and extraordinary miracles. He expects them to be concerned about what to expect during their captivity. He expects them to be concerned about being forgiven and about possibly returning to the Promised Land. He expects them to be concerned about who God really is and whether they should believe and trust in God anymore.

8 A Second Chance

Ezra 1:1-11; 3:1–4:5

LEARNING MENU

Keeping in mind the ways your class members learn best, as well as their needs and interests, choose at least one learning segment from each of the three Dimensions.

Dimension 1: What Does the Bible Say?

(A) Add to the timeline.

- You will need Bible dictionaries and art materials for class members to use to add to the timeline. Their study book and the chronology chart in this leader's guide (page 72) will also be helpful.
- Invite class members to look up the following to find dates for them. Then add these people and events to the timeline:
—Cyrus II
—Persian Empire
—first wave of people/Sheshbazzar
—second wave/Zerubbabel and Jeshua

(B) Be Bible researchers.

- Using their Bibles, Bible dictionaries and commentaries, study books, and "Additional Bible Helps," ask participants to prepare short reports on one or more of the following:
—Cyrus II
—Second Temple of Jerusalem
—Festival of Booths
—Samaritans

(C) Add to the wall map.

- Be sure the wall map of the larger Mesopotamian area is still up from Chapter 5 (or hang one: see Chapter 5, activity "A"). Leave up the map of the united monarchy if it is still on your wall. You will need a new color of yarn, pins, construction paper, scissors, felt-tip marker, and a Bible dictionary. Invite class members to look up the Persian Empire in a Bible dictionary and to study the map in their study book (inside back cover). Have them use the new yarn color to mark the boundaries of the empire on the wall map. Also have them look up in their "Glossary" the phrase *Beyond the River*, which is mentioned in Ezra 4:11.
- Possible discussion topic: How does adding another layer of boundaries to the wall map show the increasing

complexity of the whole Middle East area and the continually shifting centers of power? Refer to the map of the united monarchy, and note how Israel has gone from being a fairly great power controlling a fair amount of land in Solomon's day to becoming a vassal state within the province called Beyond the River that is controlled by a Persian king over by the Euphrates River and the Persian Gulf.

(D) Review Dimension 1 questions and answers.

- If some persons have not completed answers in their books, give them time to read the biblical passages and do so. If some have already finished their answers, they can do activities "A," "B," and/or "C."
- Review the answers quickly and invite students who did related reports to share briefly.
- Suggested answers:
  1. Cyrus is the king of Persia. He issued a decree that allowed the exiled peoples to return to their homelands and gave them a measure of religious and civic freedom. (Share report on Cyrus here if Activity "B" was done.)
  2. Cyrus decreed that the treasures that had been stolen by Nebuchadnezzar back in Josiah's day should be returned. He also commanded that the survivors not returning to Jerusalem provide them with gifts for their journey.
  3. The people first reestablished the Festival of Booths/Tabernacles (*Sukkot*) and "all the sacred festivals of the LORD" (such as Passover/Unleavened Bread [*Pesach*], and the Feast of Weeks [Pentecost/*Shavuot*]). (Share report on the Festival of Booths here if Activity "B" was done.)
  4. The people responded with both joy and sorrow when the foundation of the Temple had been laid. They sang and praised God. But the older ones wept as they remembered the first Temple. (Share report on the Second Temple here if Activity "B" was done.)
  5. These verses do not give a reason why the returning exiles refused to let the people of the land (described as "adversaries of Judah and Benjamin") help rebuild the Temple. The leader of the returning exiles simply says, "we alone will build to the LORD."

Dimension 2: What Does the Bible Mean?

(E) Discuss meanings.

- Reread the Dimension 2 material in the study book for your own understanding as teacher.

- Lead the class members in a discussion of the following questions:
  1. Why was it so important for the Israelites to go back to their ancestral lands?
  2. Some Israelites in exile obviously chose not to go back to Jerusalem to rebuild. How do you think they felt? Why do you think they did not go back?
  3. Were the Israelites who chose to stay in Babylonia making a faithful choice from the point of view of the writer of Ezra-Nehemiah? Why, or why not?
  4. Who were "the people of the land," and why were they so concerned about the returning exiles? (Share report on Samaritans, one of the groups of people of the land, here if Activity "B" was done.)

(F) Act out the Bible story.

- Read Ezra 4:1-3 aloud to the class members. Then ask each person to select a partner. When they have done so, ask them to decide which person in their team will be a returning exile and which person will be one of the people of Samaria. Ask each team to carry on a conversation the way it might have happened in verses 2 and 3 of Chapter 4. If you need to, read the three verses again to the teams and then say, "People of the land, start your conversations now." Let the teams talk a few minutes, stopping them when conversation is going well.

TEACHING TIP
Remember, people will feel more successful if you stop the activity when conversations are going strong than if you wait until the conversations fizzle.

- When you stop the conversations, ask:
  1. Those of you who played the parts of the people of the land, what points did you try to make?
  2. Those of you who played the parts of the returning exiles, what did you answer in response to the person of the land?
- Ask all the class members to reflect generally on any insights they gained about the situation that existed in 520 B.C. in Jerusalem.

(G) Visualize the new Temple.

- Invite the class members to get comfortable in their chairs (or on the floor). Suggest that they close their eyes if they wish or focus on a point on the ceiling. Tell them you are going to lead them through a brief visualization about the rebuilding of the Temple. Read the following slowly, pausing where there is a string of periods (...) to give people time to visualize.

  Let your mind travel back in history, back to the time of Jesus . . . back further to five hundred years before Jesus lived. . . . You are back in the days of King Cyrus of Persia.... You have traveled from Babylonia back to Jerusalem.... The journey was long and hard ... and when you got to Jerusalem you found the Temple in ruins.... You knew it would be in ruins; ... you remember when the Babylonians came and stole all the vessels of gold from the Temple.... You were just a little child back then, but you will never forget that time. The sight of the rubble where the Temple used to stand was very sad. Life has been hard in Jerusalem since you got back ... so much needs to be done to reclaim your life here....

But today is a day of celebration! The foundation of the Temple is to be finished today! All of us who returned from Babylonia are gathering at the Temple for a ceremony. Look, there are the priests in their vestments standing with their trumpets ... and there are the Levites with their cymbals ... and look, there are my friends.... Listen to the trumpets and the cymbals! The leaders are starting the songs of praise and thanks: "for he is good, for his steadfast love endures forever toward Israel."... We are shouting now ... shouting for joy.... I am shouting now—but then I stop. My friends are weeping; I am weeping. Our singing and praising and weeping are all one big sound ... a sound like I have never heard before........ Slowly now the sound dies away....

Slowly now bring yourself back down the centuries to the time of Jesus ... to the present time. When you are ready, open your eyes and rejoin the other class members.

- Ask several class members to share their experiences of this visualization. Ask:
—Did your find yourself transported back to Ezra's time?
—What did you "see" and "hear" and "feel"?
—What did you learn?

Dimension 3:
What Does the Bible Mean to Us?

(H) Create an imaginary conversation.

- Ask the class members to imagine that they are part of the first group who returned to the land after being exiled for many decades. Read aloud the opening paragraph of Dimension 3 in the study book.
- Set the stage for them, by saying: "You have just arrived. Where are you? What do you see and hear? What are your concerns? Your fears? Your needs? Your dreams for the future?" Give them a minute or two to visualize this silently. Then ask them to turn to a neighbor and talk. After pairs have talked a few minutes, ask several people to tell the whole class what their own visualization of a return from exile was like.

(I) Discuss meanings for us today.

- Tell class members: "Bernhard Lang, in *What the Bible Really Says*, raises the question 'to what extent is the [current] animosity between religious groups rooted in the Bible itself?' He concludes that 'if we look closely and honestly at the Hebrew Bible and the Christian New Testament, we will see that the dominant attitude toward nonbelievers is not one of integration and tolerance, but of segregation and intolerance' " (from "Segregation and Intolerance," in *What the Bible Really Says*, edited by Morton Smith and R. Joseph Hoffman; HarperSanFrancisco, 1989; page 115).
- Starter questions for discussion:
  1. What do you think about Lang's statement? What can you point to in our study of Kings, Chronicles, and now Ezra-Nehemiah that supports Lang's statement?
  2. Lang says there are places, of course, in the Bible where outsiders/outcasts are accepted. Can you point to some? Do you agree with Lang that these are exceptions rather than the rule in the Bible?
  3. If Lang is right, what does that mean for us as Christians today? about our view of the Bible? about how we use the Bible to guide our Christian lives individually and as a community?

(J) Engage in a "wise leader" debate.

- Divide class members into two groups. Give each group newsprint and markers.
- Instruct persons in the two groups to imagine they are exiles living in Babylonia. Then tell them to focus on the questions: Can we go home again? Should we try?
- Ask one group to list all the "Yes, we can and should" reasons. Ask the other group to list all the "No, we cannot and should not" reasons.
- When the groups have finished their lists, put them up on the wall in the classroom.
- If the class did Activity "K" in Chapter 1, remind them about how they acted as the ideal national leader" and the "ideal religious leader" (Chapter 1, Activity "K," page 6. Ask for two volunteers to take on the roles again, one to be the national leader and one to be the religious leader.
- Pick a current situation in the world where people are in exile from their homeland. Tell the two volunteers that they are the national and religious leaders of those people and they have just been told they can lead their people back to their homeland. What will they say to each other right after they have heard the news?
- Give the two leaders time to get the conversation going. Invite other members of the class to "coach" them. When the conversation is going well, cut it off and ask class members to reflect on the issue of "going home" or "going on where you are." What are the problems

with each in the modern world? Are there other choices?

(K) Paint a feeling-tone picture of the dilemma.

- You will need tempera paints, paint brushes, and paper. (You might be able to borrow some from the children's Sunday school classes.) You will also need old newspapers to place under sheets of paper while painting. Provide glasses of water for persons to clean their brushes as they go between different paint colors.
- Ask class members to paint an abstract picture to portray how it must have felt to the Israelites in Babylonia as they debated whether to go back to Jerusalem to try to pick up their lost lives or to keep going on with their lives in Babylonia.
- Ask several students to tell something about their paintings or about the thoughts and feelings they had while painting them.
- If not all of your participants like to paint, offer the reflection in Activity "L" along with this one. During the sharing time, invite several painters and several reflecters to share their thoughts and feelings and insights about second chances.

(L) Reflect about second chances.

- Invite class members to reflect and write about second chances in their own lives:
—What was the second chance about?
—Did you know what God wanted you to do?
—How did you know?
—Or, if you did not know clearly, how did you feel and how did you decide?
- After they have had time to write, invite several persons either to read excerpts from their writings or tell some of the thoughts and feelings they had while writing.

(M) Read "Obey My Voice," and discuss its meanings.

- Write the words to the poem (below) on a sheet of newsprint or on the board for everyone to see.
  Obey my voice
     and I will be your God
     and ye shall be My people.
  And walk in all the ways I have commanded you
     that it may be well with you
     and that I will be your God.
  Obey my voice
     and I will be your God
     and ye shall be My people.
                    (Jeremiah 7:23)

- Introduce the poem with these words: " 'Obey My Voice' is a good way to summarize what the storytellers of Kings, Chronicles, and Ezra-Nehemiah have been saying to their listeners all along. Each storyteller says obedience brings right relationship with God and prosperity and blessing to the people."
- Read the poem responsively, with one person reading the first line, half of the class members reading the second line, and the other half of the class members reading the third line. Continue with this sequence through the poem.
- Discuss: After Cyrus's edict, what did it mean for the Israelites to obey God's voice? What might this poem mean for us today as the Christian church?

Additional Bible Helps

Jerusalem and Judah in the Persian Empire
The Persian Empire came to power when Cyrus II (the Great) was victorious over his Medan overlord about 539 B.C. His empire lasted until Alexander the Great conquered the area around 330 B.C. At its height, the Persian Empire stretched from Greece in the west to India in the east and included all of the ancient lands of Israel.

During the Persian Empire the Southern Kingdom of Judah was known as *Yahud* and the people as *Yuhudites* (Judahites, or Jews). Judah was part of the Persian province known as "Beyond the River," the river being the Euphrates.

Jerusalem in Judah was in a strategic spot during the recurring conquests of this Mesopotamian area. The conquerors came from the northeast and were often in battle with Egypt to the southwest. Royal policies were dictated by economic and military needs; and it appears that Persians, like their earlier Assyrian and Babylonian counterparts, were "stationed" or relocated in the area of Jerusalem.

About Cyrus
Cyrus, the first king of Persia, was also the greatest of the kings of Persia. He rose from being a vassal within an empire that was a junior ally of Babylonia to being the greatest king of the Persian Empire, which was itself the major political "superpower" of the Mesopotamian area. It was far more extensive than the previous Assyrian or Babylonian empires, eventually even conquering Egypt.

Through his edict, Cyrus offered an element of religious tolerance. He allowed all the displaced peoples to return home, to take their gods back with them to their native places, and to build worship houses for them. (Cyrus most likely considered God a local god who resided in Jerusalem.)

Some or perhaps most of Cyrus's religious tolerance was probably carried out for a political reason. Unlike

Babylonia and Assyria who deported rebellious peoples to break up their power, Cyrus sought the peoples' loyalty by repatriating them, giving them back their gods, and giving them a measure of self-determination. Cyrus's religious tolerance appears to be way ahead of its time. He was a civil liberator who freed the Israelites, who then returned to exclusionary religious and civil practices back in Judah.

More About the Books of Ezra-Nehemiah
Several different theories exist about these two books. Readers and scholars alike have difficulty determining exact dates for events as well as establishing which kings and governors were involved. Moreover, the text of these books as we have them today appear chopped up and blended.

1. There were separate Ezra and Nehemiah memoirs of these two great leaders, one a priest/scribe and the other a governor. The Ezra memoir was Ezra 7–10 and Nehemiah 8:1–9:5. It was written in the first person, perhaps by Ezra himself. The original order may have been: Ezra 7–8, Nehemiah 8, Ezra 9–10, with Nehemiah 9:1-5 between Ezra 10:15 and 10:16. The Nehemiah memoir consisted of Nehemiah 1–7, 12:31-43 (partly), and 13:4-31 and may have been composed by him a year or so after he arrived in Jerusalem. The rest was probably added later.

One theory is that these two memoirs were combined about 400 B.C. This author added the prayer in Nehemiah 9:6-37 from the Temple archives, the pledge to keep the law in Nehemiah 10, the report of the repopulation of Jerusalem in 11:1-2, 3:20, and the expanded description of the dedication of the walls in 12:27-43.

Then later another author added Chapters 1–6 of Ezra in order to show the connections of the postexilic community to the pre-exilic one—and to provide the theological analysis that God was in charge of all this change.

2. Other scholars believe that Ezra and Nehemiah were part of the Chronicler's history and that he wrote them as an addendum to his history.

When Was Ezra Written?
Ezra's memoirs (Ezra 7–10; Nehemiah 8:1–9:5) were written while he lived. Some of these passages still remain in the first person; others were changed to third person by a later editor. One theory is that an unknown writer around 400 B.C. took Ezra's memoirs and other existing documents, like the lists of people and Cyrus's edict, and combined them with memoirs of Nehemiah and other documents into one story of Israel's two great leaders of the postexilic time. A later editor, around 300 B.C., then added Chapters 1–6 of Ezra to provide a sense of continuity with ancient Israel and Solomon's Temple.

Another theory suggests that the two books Ezra and Nehemiah were written by the Chronicler. This theory places the date of the Chronicler anywhere from the fifth to the second century, with the fourth century B.C. being most favored.

9
Ezra 9:1–10:17

Clean and Unclean

LEARNING MENU

Keeping in mind the ways your class members learn best, as well as their needs and interests, choose at least one learning segment from each of the three Dimensions.

Dimension 1: What Does the Bible Say?

(A) Add to the timeline.

- Invite class members to add the following two items to the wall timeline. They will need to make a choice about Ezra's dates or list the various options scholars propose.
—third wave of returning exiles led by Ezra
—King Darius (see 4:23-24)

(B) Study maps.

- If possible, provide a Bible dictionary or Bible atlas that shows Canaan/Palestine on several maps:
—from the days of the judges
—during the monarchy
—during the Persian Empire
- Ask class members to study the maps and prepare a brief report. Things to look for:
  1. Who was on the land when the Israelites came out of Egypt during the Exodus and settled there?
  2. Who were the neighbors of the monarchy whom Solomon conquered and ruled when his empire was at its greatest?
  3. Besides the groups discovered in the questions above, where else might the foreign wives have come from during the Persian Empire as the exiles were returning to the land of Canaan/Palestine for a second time?

(C) Research the intermarriage laws.

- You will need several different Bible dictionaries and commentaries.
- Ask persons to look up the old laws in Deuteronomy 7:1-6 and Exodus 34:11-16. Read about them in the commentaries. Also, look up the following topics in Bible dictionaries, noting what understandings of each would have been in place during Ezra's time:
—marriage
—divorce
—inheritance
—foreigner

CLEAN AND UNCLEAN 43

—guilt offerings (You might have to look under the heading of *worship* or *sacrifice*.)
- Research questions:
  1. What did Ezra 10:3 (to send them away) mean in Ezra's day?
  2. What did the old law state, and why?
  3. What probably happened to the women who were divorced by their Jewish husbands?
  4. What was the "guilt offering" mentioned in 10:19?

(D) Review Dimension 1 questions and answers.

- If some persons have not read the Bible passage and completed the answers to Dimension 1 in their study books, give them time to do so. Others might do activities "A," "B," and "C."
- Review the questions quickly and give persons a brief moment to share from activities "A," "B," and "C." Then move on to activities in Dimensions 2 and 3.
- Suggested answers:
  1. Officials tell Ezra that some of the people of Israel, including some of the priests and Levites, have "not separated from the peoples of the lands." It is unclear who these peoples were. Evidence suggests that they may have been non-Jewish women or women from Judahite families that for some reason were not recognized as part of the true remnant of God. Perhaps they were Samaritans or other Judahites who had not had the exile experience.
  2. They must be sent away because the Jewish men have mixed "the holy seed" with the people of the lands and their abominations. The holy people, the chosen people of God, have defiled themselves and been unfaithful to God.
  3. Ezra, in his prayer speaks of the people's failure to keep God's commandments. The people were told by God that "the land that you are entering to possess is a land unclean with the pollutions of the peoples of the lands." Furthermore, they were told not to marry any of the inhabitants; that is, in essence, to keep themselves "clean."
  4. The people apparently come to a decision without Ezra (who is praying) and come to tell him that they agree they have broken the ancient law of God. They covenant to send away the foreign wives and urge Ezra to be strong and do his duty.
  5. Under threat of losing their property, the people gather to hear Ezra's words. They agree to let tribal officials represent them and find out how many foreign wives are in Israel. They will then send the foreign wives and their children "away."

Dimension 2: What Does the Bible Mean?

(E) Imagine the decision.

- Divide the class members into two teams. You may wish either to place all men and all women on the two teams, or to divide men and women as evenly as possible between the two teams.
- Ask one team to brainstorm all the possible ideas, arguments, and feelings the foreign wives might have offered when they met to decide what to do about the law Ezra had reminded them of. Ask the other team to brainstorm the ideas, arguments and feelings the Jewish men (both ones who had married foreign wives and ones who had not) might have had. Ask the second group to appoint someone to deliver the conclusion in Ezra 10:3-4. When the two groups have completed their work, invite them to come together and carry on a dialogue as it might have happened long ago . . . leading to the biblical conclusion that the appointed person will deliver.
- To get them started, say: "You have just heard Ezra reading the law. You have just heard that Jewish men are not to intermarry. You look around you and see that many have foreign wives, including maybe you or your neighbors. The officials have gone to confess to Ezra this grave sin that you have committed. Here you are. What do you say to each other?"
- When the dialogue is going strong, break in and tell group members that they must deliver a decision and point to the one who was appointed beforehand to deliver the biblical decision. Then stop the imaginary dialogue; and invite people to mix up their seating, so they are not still in their planning groups.
- Discussion questions:
  1. How did it feel to be a foreign wife and realize what decision was coming?
  2. How did it feel to be a Jewish husband with a foreign wife and realize what the community was going to decide?
  3. Did anyone think about the children? How did the children feel?
  4. How did it feel to be a Jewish man or women who had obeyed the law but who had friends or neighbors who had not?

(F) Write two prayers.

- This would be a good follow-up activity to Activity "E." Invite class members to write two prayers: one from the point of view of a Jewish person and one from the point of view of a foreign wife. Ask them to assume that these prayers were prayed the night of the big decision.

- Give them time to write the prayers and then ask for several volunteers to read. Be sure you get examples of both kinds of prayers.

(G) Create more conversations.

- Print or type the situations below, and cut them apart so that a slip of paper has just one situation on it. Prepare enough so that teams of two or three can each have a slip of paper. If your class is large, make two copies of some of the situations.
- Create teams of two or three persons and give each a situation (described below). Tell them that it is now six weeks after the big decision that the people in Jerusalem made (see Ezra 10:4). The leaders are in the process of carrying out the law. Ask each team to carry on a conversation (with all the teams talking at once).
- The situations:
  1. You are wives gathered at the town well. One of you is a Samaritan woman who worships God but somewhat differently from the Judahites. You are being sent away. Your husband meets before the Council next week. You are talking to the other wives who are Jewish.
  2. You are children whose mothers are foreigners from Moab and Ammon. You and your mothers are being sent "home."
  3. You are husbands on your way to the Council. Both of you have foreign wives. One is a Judahite woman who never went into exile; the other is an Babylonian woman whose family had been forcibly relocated to Judah by the Assyrian conquerors many years ago.
  4. You are the four men who objected to the decision to send foreign wives away (see Ezra 10:15). Why did you object?
- When the conversations are going well, stop them, and invite the class members to gather together to discuss what they learned from their situations.

(H) Discuss meanings of intermarriage with foreigners.

- Discuss these questions:
  1. How would your congregation respond to the issue of intermarriage with foreigners today? What would *foreigner* mean? What would be the religious, economic, and political issues you would face if the highest bishops or religious leaders of the land suddenly called for you to obey the Deuteronomist's law?
  2. Do you see any similarities between the current struggles of the religious right and the religious left and the old struggles of purity or tolerance in Ezra's day? How are they similar? How are they different? Does the Ezra-Nehemiah story of the return from exile shed any light on our current religious struggles to relate to each other as people of God? How, or why not?
  3. What does Ezra's response to the official's confession have to say about the relationship of prayer and social action as ways to solve serious problems? Do you agree with Ezra's approach? Why, or why not?
  4. What are some positive values promoted by a policy of purity? by a policy of tolerance?

Dimension 3: What Does the Bible Mean to Us?

(I) Explore a New Testament image of clean/unclean.

- Ask the class members to turn to Acts 10:1-43. Ask various people to read:

  Reader 1: verses 1-8   Reader 5: verses 30-33
  Reader 2: verses 9-16   Reader 6: verses 34-43
  Reader 3: verses 17-23a   Reader 7: verses 44-48
  Reader 4: verses 23b-29

- Discussion questions:
  1. What does this New Testament story have to say about the issue of *clean* and *unclean* that Ezra's people wrestled with?
  2. What does it have to say about the faithful way for us today?
  3. Is any person or group unclean to us today? What words do we use to describe them, and why? Does our session today instruct us in how to respond? How, or why not?

(J) Engage in a joint brainstorming.

- Invite the whole class to quickly call out words or phrases that we use today instead of *clean/unclean* to designate people or groups or nations that are not acceptable to us. Write all their ideas in a list on newsprint or on the board.

(K) Reflect on religious identity.

- Offer this question to the class members to reflect on in writing: How do you (or how might you) maintain a strong sense of and commitment to—your own religious identity without badmouthing or excluding other peoples' religious identity and practices?
- Give them time to write. Then invite several to share insights they gained while writing.

(L) Create cinquain (sihn-CANE) poems on exclusiveness and tolerance.

- The cinquain poem form comes from France. It has five lines in the pattern at the top of the next page.

Line 1: a noun that serves as title
one word
Line 2: describes the title
two words
Line 3: action words (verbs) or
a phrase about the title
three words
Line 4: describes a feeling about the title
four words
Line 5: a word that means the same
thing as the title
one word

- If students are having trouble, suggest several work together to create one poem.

A CINQUAIN
Tolerance
lenient stance
accepting, including, absorbing
accepting you as equal
Inclusivity

(M) Create banners.

- You will need poster board or cloth pieces for the banners, as well as markers, scraps, colored construction paper, or whatever art materials you want the class members to use to create a banner. These can be permanent banners or more temporary ones from paper items.
- Invite the class members to work in teams to create one or more banners portraying the image of exclusiveness dissolving into religious tolerance. To get them started, ask them what images or symbols they might use for exclusiveness and what ones for tolerance. Then ask, "How will you show the one changing or dissolving into the other?"
- Remind them that banners usually have only a few big strong images. Sometimes they have one or two words, sometimes no words.

(N) Write prayers about exclusiveness and tolerance.

- This activity will work best as the last activity of your session.
- Invite the class members to write a prayer of their own about exclusiveness and tolerance. As they are finishing that prayer, suggest that they try writing a second one from the point of view of someone today who is excluded from the church. (If you have members in your class who would be excluded in other churches, they probably wrote the first prayer from the excluded point of view; suggest that they write their second one as one who is not excluded).
- When members are finished, invite them into a circle to actually pray their prayers. Not all persons will want to pray their prayers aloud; so tell the group that after some have prayed, you will offer a prayer and then they will sit in silence so others can offer their prayers silently.

Additional Bible Helps

Foreign Wives

"From the beginning Canaanite, Hittite, Moabite, Midianite, Ammonite, Amorite, Philistine, Egyptian, and Cushite women, as well as Hebrew women, married Hebrew men. . . .

"From the very beginning the prohibition against marrying outside the Hebrew tradition was virtually ignored. Patriarchs, leaders, ordinary men all took non-Hebrew wives. Note Esau's Hittite wives, Judith and Basemath; Judah's Canaanite wife, Bathshua; Joseph's Egyptian wife, Asenath; Zipporah, the Midianite wife of Moses, and his second wife, the enigmatic Cushite; Samson's Philistine wife; Ruth the Moabite who married Boaz; and a legion of other women, including the hundreds of alien women in Solomon's royal harem. The paradox continued for centuries: foreign women who were continually disparaged continued to marry Hebrew men. . . .

"Women of other cultures were often identified with idolatry and that is really why they were despised and feared. It had been assumed that as wives they would adopt the religion of their husbands, but their own religious practices continued to flourish through the centuries and no doubt exercised some influence on their husbands and their children. For this reason the prophets and other writers spoke scathingly against them and strong indictments of intermarriage became prevalent. In order to preserve the cultural and religious identity of the community in post-Exilic Israel, Ezra and Nehemiah excommunicated those families who refused to dismiss their foreign wives. In one sense the severity of the threat posed by the wives is an indication of the influence these women had, particularly on their husbands. . . . Husbands may have owned their wives, but religion seems to have been one area that remained beyond their control. These women were blamed for all that was wrong in Israel and were constantly held up as the cause of the sin of Hebrew men and the apostasy of the nation. . . . It is especially revealing to note that after marrying into the culture, birthing its heroes, and being part of the tradition for generation upon generation, individual women continued to be remembered as 'foreign' wives."

(From *WomanWisdom: A Feminist Lectionary and Psalter: Women of the Hebrew Scriptures: Part One*, by Miriam Therese Winter; Crossroad, 1991; pages 253–54.)

SAMPLE TIMELINE FOR SESSIONS 5 THROUGH 9

If you have chosen to do the Timeline activity during each class session so far, your class members have been developing a timeline with dates for key events. The appearance of your timeline makes no difference; the sample one below happens to move vertically. However, you may wish to check the dates in the sample timeline. They represent consensus opinions among today's biblical scholars.

All the dates on this timeline are "B.C." or "Before Christ." Keep in mind that the numbering of years before Christ runs backwards. The year 1000 B.C. is earlier than the year 950 B.C.

The abbreviation *c.* in front of a date stands for the Latin word *circa*, which mneans "approximately."

Date	Event	Session
*c.*1020–1000	Saul's reign	Session 6, Learning Activity "D"
722–721	Assyrian invasion	
721	Fall of Samaria	Session 5, Learning Activity "B"
640–609	King Josiah	
c. 621	Hulda the prophetess	
610–595	Pharaoh Neco	Session 7, Learning Activity "B"
587–586	Fall of Jerusalem	Session 5, Learning Activity "B"
550–530	Cyrus II	Session 8, Learning Activity "A"
6th–4th centuries	Persian Empire	Session 6, Learning Activity "D"; Session 8, Learning Activity "A"
538	End of the Exile	Session 6, Learning Activity "D"
538	First wave of people/Shashbazzar	Session 8, Learning Activity "A"
522–486	King Darius	Session 9, Learning Activity "A"
520–515	Second wave of people/Zerubbabel and Jeshua	Session 8, Learning Activity "A"
458	Third wave of returning exiles led by Ezra	Session 9, Learning Activity "A"

10 Walls That Divide

Nehemiah 1:1-4; 2:1-8; 6:1–7:4

LEARNING MENU

Keeping in mind the ways your class members learn best, as well as their needs and interests, choose at least one learning segment from each of the three Dimensions.

Dimension 1: What Does the Bible Say?

(A) Add to the timeline.

- You will need a Bible dictionary and art materials for class members to use in order to add the following three items to the wall timeline:
  —Nehemiah and the fourth wave of return
  —King Artaxerxes I
  —King Artaxerxes II

(B) Add to the map.

- On the large map of the empires that class members have been marking, ask them to locate Susa (one of the capitals of the Persian Empire where our story of Nehemiah begins). Mark Susa with a large arrow.
- Also invite persons to locate the three districts (Samaria, Ammon, and Arabia) neighboring Judah whose governors were enemies of Nehemiah. See Nehemiah 2:10; 4:1-7; 6:1-9.

(C) Research the walls of Jerusalem.

- You will need Bible dictionaries for persons to read about the wall. Use the "Additional Bible Helps," page 51, for your own study or give a copy to class members to help with their research.
- Ask persons to look up *Jerusalem* and *walls* in the Bible dictionaries. Have them prepare a brief report comparing the wall of Jerusalem in David's and Solomon's days with the wall as it was rebuilt by Nehemiah.
- Alternative activity or an addition to this activity: View a segment of the video in the *Bible Teacher Kit* (Abingdon, 1994; available from Cokesbury). Look especially at the part on Jerusalem (which talks about the wall) in Part 2, "Southern Palestine."

(D) Research on women in Ezra-Nehemiah's days.

- You will need Bible dictionaries and a copy of the "Additional Bible Helps," page 46. Other helpful

resources would include: *The Women's Bible Commentary*; Miriam Therese Winter's *WomanWisdom* and *WomanWitness* (two volumes on women in the Hebrew Scriptures); and William E. Phipps's *Assertive Biblical Women.* (See "Suggested Resource List," page 71.)
- Ask class members to prepare brief reports on these topics:
—What was life like for women in pioneer Israel?
—Who are the women who are mentioned in Ezra-Nehemiah (for example, the daughters of Shallum in Nehemiah 3:12; the prophetess Noadiah in Nehemiah 6:14; the queen in Nehemiah 2:6)?
—Why is the mention of women at the dedication of the second Temple important?

(E) Review questions in study book.

- If some students have not read the biblical passages and answered the questions in Dimension 1 of the study book, give them time to do so. Other students may do one or more of activities "A"–"D" or prepare the reading in activity "F." Or if you do activity "F" you might skip the review of questions since the dramatic reading will make very clear what happened.
- Quickly review the answers to the questions with the class members and hear related reports. Then move on to Dimension 2 and 3 activities that get at the heart of the biblical passages.
- Suggested answers:
  1. Nehemiah is a Jew in exile who is cupbearer to King Artaxerxes. After he receives a message from his brother Hanani that Jerusalem is in sad shape, he leads another group of exiles to Jerusalem to rebuild the wall and refortify the city. His memoirs of that mission are included in the Book of Nehemiah.
  2. Nehemiah tells his king and queen that he is sad because the city of his ancestors' graves lies wasted and in need of repair. (Some scholars speculate that he did not specifically name Jerusalem because the city was known to be rebellious. Nehemiah may have feared the king would refuse his request to refortify it. Scholars also speculate that the queen [whose name was Damaspia according to *Harper's Bible Dictionary*, page 380] was influential in helping Nehemiah return to Jerusalem.)
  3. Three governors (Sanballat of Samaria, Tobiah of Ammon, and Geshem of Arabia) plot against Nehemiah. They were governors appointed by the king of Persia just like Nehemiah was. Because they do not want the city wall rebuilt, they try to entice Nehemiah away from the city to harm him. Then they spread false rumors through a letter threatening to tell the Persian king he is preparing to rebel. Finally, they bribe at least one of the Jewish prophets (and probably more since a woman prophet is also mentioned in Nehemiah 6:14) to give him false warnings.
  4. Nehemiah refuses to leave the city, tells them they are making up lies about him, and finally refuses to follow the advice of his prophet to hide in the Temple. He wins over his enemies and the wall is finally completed.

Dimension 2: What Does the Bible Mean?

(F) Do a dramatic reading of Nehemiah.

- You will need six copies of Nehemiah 6:1-16 from the same translation of the Bible. Mark the different copies for these parts:
—Nehemiah (who serves as the narrator since he tells his story in first person);
—Sanballat and Geshem (verse 2b, "Come and let . . .");
—Nehemiah's messengers (verse 3b, "I am doing . . ."; also 8b, "No such. . .);
—Sanballat's servant (reads the letter in verses 6-7);
—Shemaiah (verse 10, "Let us meet . . .").
- Recruit six readers when persons first arrive, and let them practice while others are doing activities "A"–"D." Ask them to designate a stage where they will sit and the audience section for the rest of the class members. After the reading, invite comments and responses. As teacher, you might offer any of the facts found in the answers to Dimension 1 questions (Activity "E") that you think were not made clear from the reading.
- Alternative ways to do this activity:
—Assign different people to read the different parts; ask the class to be Sanballat's servant and read the letter in verses 6-7.
—Instead of doing the story as a reading with characters standing or sitting still, designate one area of the stage for Nehemiah and another for Sanballat and a third for Geshem. Assign messengers to both governors and have them speak their lines together. Have messengers and servants move back and forth between Nehemiah and the governors.

(G) Discuss Bible meanings.

- Discuss the following questions:
—How much of the need to repair the wall and refortify the city of Jerusalem seemed to be for religious survival and how much seemed to be for security or political and economic reasons? What clues can you point to?
—Our biblical passage seems to assume that the wall of Jerusalem must be rebuilt. We are not told of any dis-

cussion or debate about the matter. Instead of rebuilding walls, what else might Nehemiah have done? What might have been the consequences if he had tried something else?

Dimension 3: What Does the Bible Mean to Us?

(H) Discuss walls today.

- Invite the class members to find the various kinds of walls mentioned in Dimension 3 of their study book. As they call them out, list them on newsprint, markerboard, or chalkboard. Then invite persons to add any other famous walls (real or symbolic) they can think of. (How about the walls of Jericho? the Mason-Dixon Line? the Berlin Wall? the Great Wall of China?)
- Starter discussion questions:
  1. How might the world be different if there had never been walls?
  2. What if walls were not allowed to be built for fortification? What problems would we have to solve differently in today's world?
  3. Do you think the strong biblical voice of God demanding purity/exclusiveness has caused more harm or more good over the centuries since Nehemiah lived? How? Why?
  4. What would have to change in our society for us to get rid of symbolic walls like the glass ceiling for women or the tendencies of people to want their neighborhoods to be exclusively one kind of people?
  5. What positive, good functions can walls perform? Are there some walls that we should not want to rid ourselves of?

(I) Explore wise leader characteristics again.

- Recall for class members the activities on ideal or wise leaders (in Chapters 1 and 8). Review Nehemiah's responses when he is presented with problems (in Nehemiah 1 and 6). Ask the class members to appoint two representatives from the religious leader team and the national leader team that they set up in Chapter 8.
- Invite the two leaders to discuss Nehemiah as a leader and whether he was wise.

> **TEACHING TIP**
> This activity will not work well unless the class members have done the "ideal or wise leader" activities in previous chapters ("K" in Chapter 1; "J" in Chapter 8). If you did not do them then, go back and pick up the activity of creating the wise leader traits. Then skip to the activity above.

(J) Create cinquain poems.

- The cinquain (sihn-CANE) poem comes from France. It has five lines in the pattern shown below:
  Line 1: a noun that serves as title
  one word
  Line 2: describes the title
  two words
  Line 3: action words (verbs) or a phrase about the title
  three words
  Line 4: describes a feeling about the title
  four words
  Line 5: a word that means the same thing as the title
  one word

> **TEACHING TIP**
> If students are having trouble, suggest several work together to create one poem.
> If some students like to write and some like to create art, offer activity "K" at the same time as this poem-writing one.

> **A CINQUAIN**
> Wall
> iron curtain
> enclosing, dividing, fortifying
> desperately blocking our connection
> Barrier

(K) Create a montage of walls.

- Collect an array of magazines (old *National Geographics* or travel magazines would be good). You will also need colored construction paper, white drawing paper, colored markers, and glue or paste. Provide a long sheet of butcher paper (or some of your church's paper tablecloth paper).
- Suggest that the long sheet of paper represents a "wall" and invite students to create a montage (a composite picture where some pictures are partly laid over others in an attractive and meaningful way) of walls in their lives or in others' lives. Suggest that they decide on a title for the montage, something like "Walls That Support/Walls That Divide." They will need to determine where they want them to go before they start gluing pictures on. The construction paper and markers are for them to draw their own pictures if they cannot find a photo or drawing in magazines.
- Alternative way: If you do not need to offer this activity

along with the poem activity, consider offering it when persons first arrive for this session. It will get them thinking about walls in their lives.

(L) Reflect about walls.

- Ask class members to reflect in writing about walls in their own lives—real walls and symbolic walls, walls that connect and support our living and walls that separate and disrupt our lives.
- When they have had time to reflect and write, invite several to share excerpts or to reflect on insights they gained from writing.

(M) Discover the walls in our cities.

- Introduce this activity by reading the following "news item":
    "Evanston, Illinois, is a suburb north of Chicago. The boundary line between them is Howard Street. In 1993, Evanston decided to build a new shopping mall on its side of Howard Street. Residents on the Chicago side got upset about possible increased traffic, crime, nuisance, and so on. So, Chicago residents talked to their alderman who then initiated the construction of a 2 1/2 foot-high metal barrier (a low wall!) right down the middle of Howard street" (paraphrased and summarized from an article in *The Evanston Review*; September 22, 1994; page 5).
- Explore the issues and concerns in this scenario. Identify similar situations in your community.
- Invite the class members to share similar events in their own experience. Use their events and/or the Chicago-Evanston story to explore what attitudes were involved and what other attitudes might have been assumed.
- Note: A circuit court judge ruled the wall had to come down. Appeals were still going on as this curriculum went to print.

(N) Create a prayer for closing.

- Create a litany prayer, using the refrain from "Walls That Divide" (page 86 in the study book) as the common litany refrain. Invite each person in class to write one line of the litany. Suggest that the prayer lines be focused on ideas from the chapter about walls and separations and barriers in our lives. Use the following as a pattern:
  God, we confess that_____, and we ask for _____.
- Another way to use these words as a closing prayer is to ask five persons each to read a stanza from this hymn (stanza 1 is in the study book, page 86; the other stanzas are printed at the top of the next column). After each reading, ask class members to read the refrain in unison.

When vested power stands firm entrenched
and breaks the burdened back,
when waste and want live side by side,
it's gospel that we lack!

Refrain:
Walls that divide are broken down,
Christ is our unity!
Chains that enslave are thrown aside
Christ is our liberty!

The truth we seek in varied scheme,
the life that we pursue,
unites us in a common quest
for self and world made new.
Refrain:

The church divided seeks that grace,
that newness we proclaim,
a unity of serving love
that lives praise to God's name.
Refrain:

This broken world seeks lasting health
and vital unity,
God's people, by God's word renewed,
cast off all slavery![1]
Refrain:

---

[1]"Walls That Divide," by Ron Klusmeier and Walter Farquharson in *Everflowing Streams;* The Pilgrim Press, 1981; page 59.

- When the prayer is done, use it as the closing for this session.

Additional Bible Helps

Old Testament Uses of Walls
In Old Testament days, farmers regularly cleared fields for planting crops by removing unwanted stones and using them to build low stone walls around the edges of the fields. Stone-walled terraces were built for vineyards and orchards.

Houses were built of rough stones or mudbricks set on a stone foundation. Walls of houses were sometimes covered with a coating of plaster. The more important public and religious buildings, like the Temple, were built of carefully shaped (hammer-dressed) stones. Larger buildings also often were built with wooden beams.

City walls were fortifications that included walls, towers, and gates. They were up to fifteen feet thick. Some walls were built of solid stones piled on each other with mortar to hold them. Others were "casemate" walls that consisted of two parallel walls separated by five or six feet of empty space and periodic crosswalls to strengthen them.

The average area enclosed by a city wall in ancient Israel was five to ten acres. Under Solomon's reign, however, Jerusalem's walls were extended to a thirty-two-acre city. Later, in the eighth century, the enclosed part of Jerusalem was enlarged even further when a wall was added to enclose the Mishneh, the western hill area of Jerusalem.

Two interesting facts about walled cities: the oldest known fortified town in ancient Israel is Jericho (about 7000 B.C.); the next known fortified towns (like Gezer and Megiddo) were built some four thousand years later.

Another View on Rebuilding Walls

"The first *task* in our transformation is the rebuilding of the city wall. The city wall of Jerusalem distinguished what was inside the city from what was outside. It helped the city establish its identity. So for us in our congregational life. We must clarify what makes us different, so that we can undertake our vocation as apostles. This requires us to establish the authenticity and distinctiveness of our congregations so that we live visibly in our faith, shaped by the biblical heritage, not by the least common denominator of local values and morality. We must build congregations where people know and follow Jesus, not the latest polls.

"Those congregations must become centers that can provide space for genuine encounter, where one may be confronted and supported in the deep experiences of life. These congregations must be communities that can help each of us discover our gifts and our special vocation to serve our society. Rebuilding the wall means clarifying the boundary of the community and continuing to maintain it. It involves getting clearer and clearer about what is inside and what is not inside the community. In our tradition it means actively welcoming those who come to the congregation, but carefully training them in the stories of the faith.

"Within our tradition, the wall, the boundary, is not for the purpose of separation but of service. The function of the boundary is not to exclude but to help the community strengthen its identity and its commitment to serving. The purpose of the community is to increase its ability for each to reach out beyond the boundary. The integrity of the wall is to help the community in its continuing effort to discern its mission and that of each member.

"Congregations, following the example of those who returned from exile in Babylon, have first the task of rebuilding the city wall so that the people can once again grasp their identity in this alien and confusing world. The wall defines the community that sends its members out in service and receives them back for healing and nurture. The wall is to help the community intensify its thrust out beyond the wall.

"We are called to reestablish the boundary between the congregations and the society around them, getting clear about the cultural distance between followers of the values of this world and followers of the gospel. We are powerless to change ourselves and the world if we are confused about what our community stands for."

From *Transforming Congregations for the Future*, by Loren B. Mead; The Alban Institute, 1994; pages 115–16.

11
Two Women—Two Choices

Esther 1:10-22; 2:15-23

LEARNING MENU

Keeping in mind the ways your class members learn best, as well as their needs and interests, choose at least one learning segment from each of the three Dimensions.

Dimension 1: What Does the Bible Say?

(A) Add to the wall map.

- Be sure the wall map of the Assyrian Empire (which was first suggested in Chapter 5) is still on the wall, or put one up if you have not done so before. Also you will need a Bible dictionary, yarn, and pins.
- If class members did not mark Susa (the winter residence of the king of Persia) in the last session, have them do it now. Ask them to use the Bible dictionary (look up *Persia*; also check maps) to locate the boundaries of the Persian Empire. Ask them to compare their findings with Esther 1:1 and then to use the yarn to mark roughly the outline of King Ahasuerus's empire.

(B) Add to the timeline.

- You will need a Bible dictionary, one or two commentaries on Esther, and art materials to use for adding to the timeline.
- Ask class members to research dates for the following and add them to the wall timeline:
—King Xerxes I (also called Artaxerxes I or Ahasuerus) (Note: Students may have already put this king on the timeline in Session 10.);
—Vashti, Esther, and Mordecai;
—Book of Esther (date written);
—Additions to Esther as found in the Apocrypha (when written).
   Note: Scholars disagree about dates for the Book of Esther and for the Additions, so persons will need to indicate alternatives on the timeline.

(C) Discover the two versions of Esther.

The purpose of this activity is to help class members visualize what the six Additions to Esther are and how they fit into the basic story. The chart that the class members prepare should be kept; it will be referred to again in Chapter 13.

- You will need a Bible dictionary, a study Bible with the Apocrypha (which has the Additions to Esther), several

commentaries on Esther, large sheets of newsprint or butcher paper, and two colors of felt-tipped markers.
- Ask class members to use the Bible dictionary, commentaries, and study Bible to discover the Additions to Esther (the Greek version of Esther). Once they have figured out what the six additions are, ask them to create an outline of Esther with one color of marker and to show where the additions fit in with the second color.
- A good way to do this would be in two columns. In the left column list the basic Hebrew version of Esther (by chapters/verses and a very brief phrase summarizing that portion of the story. In the right column (which will start first, since Addition A comes before the Hebrew 1:1) list the letter (A, B, C, D, E, F) of the addition and a brief phrase about the content of the addition.
- If a small group does this activity, ask them to be prepared to present the chart to the whole class later in the session.

> **TEACHING TIP**
> The "answer" to this activity is on page 57. You may be tempted to copy that chart and give it to class members. However, they will visualize the two versions much better if they have to hunt up the information and write it out themselves! You can use the "answer chart" to give them hints if they get stuck.

(D) Review questions in the study book.

- If some students have not answered the questions in their study book, give them time when they arrive. Other students can do one or more of activities "A," "B," and "C." Review the questions and answers quickly. Give class members time to present learnings from the map, timeline, and research activities.
- Answers to questions in study book:
  1. Queen Vashti was commanded by the king to appear before his all-male banquet wearing her crown (and perhaps only her crown). The king wanted to display her beauty before them. Queen Vashti refused.
  2. The king wanted to know what to do with his independent queen. The king's officials saw a larger problem. They knew that the women had heard Vashti refuse. Because of that, the officials were afraid that their own wives and other men's wives would follow Vashti's example and refuse to obey various commands given by the men. They knew they needed to make an "example" of Vashti to give a clear message to all women that refusing a husband's command would bring quick and harsh punishment.
  3. Esther was adopted by her uncle Mordecai (who "sits at the king's gate" as a royal courtier). The implication of the Scripture is that Mordecai pressed Esther to join the harem. Once in the harem, she was very adaptive to the routines. She seemingly is not concerned about abandoning her Jewish heritage and its dietary laws, nor does she reveal her Jewish heritage. She quickly learns to follow the eunuch Hegai's advice. Her compliance with harem life along with her beauty and ability to please the king sexually earn her the position of Queen of Persia.
  4. Mordecai uncovers a plot by two eunuchs to assassinate the king. Queen Esther, now in a more powerful position, uses her position within the royal structure and the male-dominated culture to enhance her Uncle Mordecai's status. She reports Mordecai's discovery. The eunuchs are killed and the event is recorded in the royal records, with Mordecai being given credit for the discovery.

Dimension 2:
What Does the Bible Mean?

(E) Discuss some hard decisions.

- Use the following questions to explore further the story of Vashti. After reviewing Esther 1:10-22, discuss:
  1. What else might Vashti have done to make her point?
  2. What might the officials have done differently?
  3. What message might Jewish women reading the Book of Esther have learned from the story of Queen Vashti? What might Christian women today learn?

(F) Explore different points of view.

The purpose of this activity is to help the class members get "inside" the characters of the story and discover what their possible assumptions were. Remember, we only know from the biblical story what one point of view was. It is possible, for example, that some officials and women involved in the story might have held different assumptions.

- Divide class members into four groups. The groups can be mixed women and men. Assign the groups to the following task after they review Esther 1:1-22:
  Group 1: explore the king's assumptions;
  Group 2: explore the officials' assumptions;
  Group 3: explore Queen Vashti's assumptions;
  Group 4: explore the banquet women's assumptions (remember, they overheard Vashti refusing the king).
- Give each group time to discuss the story and their character's part in it. Emphasize that they are to try to identify their character's assumptions (or beliefs) about men, women, and power. Groups 2 and 4 of course might have several different assumptions. Give each group newsprint and markers to list the assumptions they identify.

- If groups are having trouble getting started, give them the following examples:
—The king: "Women exist only for his pleasure."
—One of the women at the banquet: "Women are better off if they just do what men want."
—Another woman: "Women need to assert their independence more."
—An official: "Men are natural leaders" and "women need to be led and controlled."
—Any one of the characters: "Mostly this society works, so women shouldn't rock the boat."
- When groups have made their lists, quickly divide each group into two subgroups: A and B. (That is, half of group 1 goes into subgroup A and half into subgroup B; half of group 2 goes to subgroup A and half to subgroup B, and so on.)
- Note: If you have more than sixteen people, have the original groups divide into four new subgroups: A, B, C, D.
- Ask the new groups (which now have representatives of the king, Vashti, officials, and women) to carry on an imaginary conversation in character.
- The question they are to discuss is: Was Vashti right or wrong to do what she did?
- Remind the groups that the assumptions they originally identified on newsprint will help them know how to "play their character."
- When the discussions are going strong, cut them off and ask class members to become themselves again. Then use the following questions to explore the issues of men, women, and power:
  1. While you were playing your character, how did you feel about the other men and women?
  2. Which assumptions and arguments made sense to you? Why?
  3. Which assumptions and arguments did not make sense to you? Why?

(G) Compare Esther's approach to Vashti's.

- You will need to gather plenty of sheets of newsprint and three different colored markers.
- Put up two sheets of newsprint. Title one sheet "Esther" and the other sheet "Vashti."
- Ask class members to call out all the characteristics of the style and approach used by Esther as seen so far in Chapters 1 and 2 of the Book of Esther (for example, obeys men, uses her beauty to get what she wants, and so on).
- Then ask them to call out all the characteristics of the style and approach used by Vashti.
- Ask class members to study both lists and to call out the items that are positive ones. With a second color marker, put a plus (+) for each item that is positive.

Finally, ask them to call out items that are negative and put a minus (-) beside them in a third color marker. You may end up with several marks next to an item if class members disagree.
- Give class members a little time to look at the results. Ask them to reflect on what they see. Then ask them to discuss:
—Would they agree with some scholars who have labeled Vashti feminist and Esther feminine?
—Is one woman more positive or negative for your class members? Why, or why not?

Dimension 3: What Does the Bible Mean to Us?

(H) Brainstorm a list of modern Vashtis.

- Quickly call out or list on newsprint other groups today (besides women) who like Vashti must live within the structures and under the rules made by others.

(I) Reflect on power and relationships.

- List the following questions on chalkboard, marker board, or newsprint.
  1. Who is "the king" in my life?
  2. Is there any of the "king" in me?
  3. Who are "the officials" in my life?
  4. Is there any of the "officials" in me?
  5. Am I more like Vashti or Esther?
- Invite class members to reflect in writing on these questions.
- After they have had time to write, invite those who wish to share briefly to do so.

(J) Explore understandings of patriarchy.

- Question for discussion: How does the story of Vashti help you understand the idea of patriarchy?
- Share definitions of patriarchy from the sidebar below to get this discussion going.

DEFINITIONS OF PATRIARCHY

- "A social system in which the father is the head of the family and descent is traced through the father's side of the family; a family, community, or society based on this system or governed by men" (from *The American Heritage Dictionary of the English Language*, third edition; Houghton Mifflin Company, 1992; page 1328).

> • "In its narrow meaning, patriarchy refers to the system, historically derived from Greek and Roman law, in which the male head of the household had absolute legal and economic power over his dependent female and male family members. People using the term that way often imply a limited historicity for it; patriarchy began in classical antiquity and ended in the nineteenth century with the granting of civil rights to women and married women in particular.
>
> "This usage is troublesome because it distorts historical reality. The patriarchal dominance of male family heads over their kin is much older than classical antiquity; it begins in the third millennium B.C. and is well established at the time of the writing of the Hebrew Bible. Further, it can be argued that in the nineteenth century male dominance in the family simply takes new forms and is not ended. . . .
>
> "***Patriarchy*** in its wider definition means the manifestation and institutionalization of male dominance over women and children in the family and the extension of male dominance over women in society in general. It implies that men hold power in all the important institutions of society and that women are deprived of access to such power. It does *not* imply that women are either totally powerless or totally deprived of rights, influence, and resources" (*The Creation of Patriarchy*, by Gerda Lerner; Oxford University Press, 1986; pages 238–39).

(K) Identify current systems of patriarchy.

- You will need five or six sheets of newsprint, three markers, and a timer that can be set for three minutes and that makes a sound when time is up.
- Divide the class members into a men's group and a women's group. Ask each group to list on newsprint specific examples of patriarchy in operation in our relationships, our churches, and our society. If you have not already done so, share information about the meaning of *patriarchy* from the sidebar above.
- Then bring the two groups together and ask them to build a common list of how patriarchy works today.
- Start out by having one group read one of their examples. If the other group agrees, write it on a sheet of newsprint on which you have printed the title "Commonly Agreed Upon Examples of Modern Patriarchy at Work." If the other group disagrees the two groups will need to negotiate different wording. Give them three minutes (set the timer). When the bell rings, if they cannot agree, then the item does not go on the common list. Go on to the next item (proposed by the other group).

   Note: To build this common list persons will need to listen to each other carefully and perhaps negotiate with each other on how something is identified and worded. If both groups cannot agree, the item stays on the small group list.
- Debriefing questions:
  1. How did you feel doing this activity? (Many will be uncomfortable. Affirm that this is OK. Naming our different understandings to each other is not always easy.)
  2. What did you learn about yourself and others of your gender by doing this activity?
  3. What did you learn about the other gender by doing this activity?
  4. How did the negotiating process work for you?

(L) Create a closing prayer.

- As a class, create a prayer that
  1. confesses our human tendency to seek "power over" others, and
  2. asks for God's help as we try to create "power with" or "power equal" relationships between men and women.
- Print the prayer on newsprint or board.
- Use it as the closing activity for this session.
- Alternative way: If your class is large, you might divide into two groups and have one group write the confession part (1.) and the other group write the petition part (2.). Then have them pray the entire prayer together at the end of the session.

Additional Bible Helps

What's in a Name?

The Hebrew form of the name *Esther* is *Hadassah*, which means "myrtle." Esther is probably a Babylonian or Persian name given to her in the royal court. The name *Esther* may be derived from the Persian word *stara* or star. It may be a form of the name *Ishtar*, a goddess in the Akkadian pantheon who was widely worshiped in Mesopotamia from earliest times until at least first century B.C. *Ishtar* came to be a general noun meaning "goddess." It was related to specific goddess names like Astarte and Athtar.

Two similarities contribute to seeing a possible connection between the names *Ishtar* and *Esther*. Ishtar was celebrated as a goddess of war and Esther waged war (on Israel's enemies who may well have worshiped Ishtar). Ishtar was known for her eroticism, and Esther was known for her great beauty and ability to please the king sexually.

Mordecai, the name of Esther's cousin, may be a form of *Marduk* or *Marduka*. Marduk was a Persian Babylonian god. Ancient records identify a Marduka in the court of Xerxes I.

TWO VERSIONS OF ESTHER (ANSWER CHART FOR "C")

HEBREW ESTHER	SIX ADDITIONS
	A. Mordecai's dream and first plot to assassinate the king.
1:1–3:13 Vashti's refusal and dismissal as queen of Persia; Esther becomes new queen. Haman is promoted; Mordecai refuses to bow down; Haman plots against Jews.	
	B. King's letter ordering the massacre of the Jews.
3:14–4:17 Letter is posted; Mordecai mourns and seeks Esther's aid; Esther finally agrees.	
	C. Prayers of Mordecai and Esther.
5:1-2 Esther invites king and Haman to a private dinner.	
	D. Expansion of 5:1-2; appeal to king, with added religious elements.
5:3–8:12 Esther's banquets; Haman's boasting and plot; king honors Mordecai; Haman fumes; Esther's appeal to save her people and accusation of Haman; Haman's terror and hanging; Mordecai identified as Esther's cousin, promoted to Haman's place; Esther and Mordecai's plan to save the Jews.	
	E. King's second letter, denouncing Haman, directing loyal Persians to help Jews.
8:13–10:3 New royal letter is sent naming day for Jewish defense; Jews kill enemies, including Haman's sons; Esther gets second day for killing enemies; after killings, the Jews celebrate. Purim is established, justified, validated in biblical records.	
	F. Mordecai's dream is interpreted as God's divine intervention; and the Book of Esther is claimed to be genuine.

Two Women—Two Choices

12
Esther 3:1-11; 4:4-17; 7:2-6a; 8:5-12

Upsetting the Balance

LEARNING MENU
Keeping in mind the ways your class members learn best, as well as their needs and interests, choose at least one learning segment from each of the three Dimensions.

Dimension 1: What Does the Bible Say?

(A) Research the enmity between Haman and Mordecai.

- Ask early-arriving class members to use a Bible dictionary to look up the entries: *Haman*, *Mordecai*, and *Agag*. Ask them also to read 1 Samuel 15.
- Discuss:
—Why were the Benjaminites and the Agagites ancient enemies?
—How does the action of Saul five centuries earlier help explain why Mordecai will not bow down to Haman?

(B) Identify the dramatic "reversals" in Esther.

- You will need newsprint or markerboard and a marker or a chalkboard and chalk.
- Ask participants to look through Chapters 3 through 8 of Esther and list on newsprint or board the verses where a "reversal" of some kind takes place. If a small group is doing this activity, ask them to prepare a short report for the whole class.
- If persons have trouble identifying "reversals" share the following example: In 6:9-10, Haman expects to be honored by the king; but then he discovers that Mordecai is the one to be honored.
- Note: If you ask a group to work on this activity, you may wish to invite them to report either at the beginning of activity "I" or "D."

(C) Look at another "court intrigue" story in the Bible.

- On a sheet of paper or on newsprint, print the following parallel Bible verses:
  Esther 2:8-12   Daniel 1:3-9
  Esther 3:1-12   Daniel 2:1-13
  Esther 7:3-4   Daniel 2:14-16

- Share with participants that the Book of Daniel was written by a devout Jew living in a time of Jewish persecution (167–164 B.C.) and that he told the stories in the Book of Daniel to give Jews hope that if they were faithful they would triumph over their enemies. These stories contain a similar kind of court intrigue as in Esther. However, Daniel shows his Jewish faith in more obvious ways than Esther did.
- Ask class members to compare the two stories, answering these questions:
  1. Where are they similar and how are they different?
  2. How does Daniel show his Jewish faith and how does Esther seem to ignore hers?
- If you ask a group to work on this activity, request that they prepare a brief report to share with the class.

(D) Review the questions in the study book.

- If persons need to finish answering questions in their study book, suggest that they do so when they first arrive. Other students can work on activities "A," "B," or "C."
- Quickly review the questions and invite students to briefly share learnings from activities "A," "B," and "C."
- Answers to the study book questions:
  1. Haman is furious that Mordecai will not bow down. Haman reacts by deciding to kill all the Jews in Persia. He determines a day for the mass destruction and gets the king to approve a public decree announcing the day of killing.
  2. Queen Esther has to decide whether to remain the properly compliant and obedient Persian queen or to risk her own death in order to gain an audience with the king and influence him to save her people.
  3. Finally, after a second banquet night where Esther has been the proper and beautiful hostess, and when she is sure that the king is quite enamored of her, she tells him that she wants him to save her and her people. She reveals Haman as the one who has planned to have her killed.
  4. Having Haman killed and Mordecai installed in his place still does not solve the problem because Haman's decree (sealed with the king's ring) still stands: the Jews are still to be killed at the end of the year. So Esther tearfully pleads with the king to change the decree. She very subtly (in 8:5) implies that the decree was not really the king's anyway; it was "devised by Haman" whom the king has just executed. Persian law forbids the revoking of a king's decree, but the king generously tells Esther and Mordecai that if they can write something to get around it, they are free to do so and can use his ring to make it a royal decree.

Dimension 2:
What Does the Bible Mean?

(E) Pantomime the story.

- If you want class members to act out the story with a little realism, collect a few props, such as something to represent "sackcloth," a bundle of "clothes," something to identify the banquets (perhaps a candle and candleholder), a ring, a scroll. If you have them pantomime the story, you may not need any props.
- Ask class members to volunteer for parts (or if time is short, just assign them quickly). Begin the drama at 4:1 and end at 8:17, but tell actors to dramatize the high points! Give them a few minutes to "study" their parts. Then ask them to pantomime the main actions of the story.
- Options: Rather than pantomiming the major actions of the story, persons might act out the story while you as teacher read the major action sections. If you have more time, they might act it out and create their own dialogue to portray the story.
- Major parts include: King Ahasuerus, Esther, Mordecai, and Haman. Minor parts (which could be played by the same two or three people) include: Esther's maids and eunuchs, Haman's wife and friends, king's secretaries and courtiers.
- After the play take a few minutes to let class members talk about how they felt doing the play. Also ask them to reflect on whether they gained any new insights into the story of Esther by acting it out.

(F) Discuss the story further.

- Use the following questions to explore the main plot of the story of Esther:
  1. Compare the decisions that Esther and Vashti had to make to stand up to the king. Is one decision or cause more worthy than the other?
  2. Compare the two men Haman and Mordecai. What is the major personal characteristic of each in your opinion? They are cast as villain and hero. Is there any good in Haman? any bad in Mordecai?
  3. What "assets" does Esther use to accomplish her goals? (Esther still acts within the patriarchal system, as opposed to Vashti who directly challenges it. Esther uses food, feminine beauty, the king's pleasure, Haman's self-conceit, and so on, to accomplish her own ends.)

(G) Find out what Esther is like.

- For this activity you will need several commentaries on the Book of Esther (see the "Suggested Resource List," page 71, for possibilities, and check with your pastor and church library for availability).
- Invite class members to browse through the various commentaries. Ask them to note especially how Esther is described as a person. Ask class members to be prepared to discuss the similarities and differences found among the commentaries.
- After time for browsing, ask class members to report on their findings.
- Possible discussion questions:
—Do some commentaries give a more positive slant on Esther than others? Why?
—Do some commentaries make her more real? Why?
—If you did not find any differences, why do you think there was not any difference? (Were all your commentaries older ones? or written from the same perspective?)

(H) Examine Esther's approach in the patriarchy.

- Tell class members: "In the last session, we began to compare Vashti's approach and Esther's approach within the same patriarchal system. Today in this activity we will look more closely at Esther's decisions."
- Invite class members to look for additional evidence of Esther's approach in Chapters 3–8 in the Bible. List characteristics on newsprint (add to the list started last session). Once the list is completed, use the following questions to get discussion started.
  1. What compromises has Esther had to make to get along in her male-controlled world?
  2. What causes her to take a stand against the system?
  3. What caused Vashti to take a stand against the system?
  4. How does Esther's "cause" differ from Queen Vashti's (which we can only speculate about)?
  5. Is Esther's cause a "better" one than Vashti's? Is Vashti's better than Esther's?

(I) Explore the reversals of power.

- If persons did activity "B" earlier, ask them to report their findings now. Then ask them to identify which of the reversals were reversals of the existing balance of power. (Use a colored marker to put a big "P" [for Power] beside those. Put an "O" [for Other] beside those which indicate some other kind of reversal.)
- Examine the reversals of balance of power more closely and discuss the following:
  1. What was going on?
  2. How did the power change?
  3. Was it for better or for worse? for whom?

TEACHING TIP
Reversals

The major reversals in power in the story are:
- Vashti loses power when she was deposed as queen and Esther gains power as she becomes queen. (One question to explore with the class is whether Vashti gained any personal power by her choice.)
- Esther gains power temporarily over Mordecai as she takes charge and Mordecai becomes more passive. Yet in the end, Esther restores power to Mordecai. (One question to explore is how and why that flow of power happened between Esther and Mordecai.)
- Haman gains power and then loses it to Mordecai. (Did Haman gain power "legitimately"? What things caused Haman to lose his power (what things inside himself and what things outside in the "system")?
- The king has power but keeps giving it away (to his officials in Chapter 1, to Haman in Chapter 3, to Esther in Chapters 5 and 7, and to Esther and Mordecai in Chapter 8). Why does he keep giving power away? One possible answer is that his passion for women and his love or even obsession with Esther caused him to give his power away. Do your class members agree?

Dimension 3: What Does the Bible Mean to Us?

(J) Find ways we upset the balance of power today.

- Introduce the idea that another example of a modern-type Esther story is the story of the underground railroad movement in the United States during slavery years. Ask the class to think of parallels between the story of Esther saving her Jewish people and the people who ran the underground railroad.
- Discussion questions:
  1. Could Esther have run an "underground railroad" of some kind to save the Jews? Why? Why not?
  2. Besides the underground railroad movement, what other things do people do to try to change the balance of power in today's world? (Protest movements and demonstrations; election processes, lobbying, writing books, becoming a radio or TV talk show host or hostess, filibustering in Congress, assassinations of leaders, buying influence with money or other bribes, creating documentary films and videos.)
  3. What would have to change in our world for protest movements and so on to become unnecessary? (Note: this question could have two kinds of answers: total

dictatorships or genuine equality for all people and a new kind of use of "power-with" rather than "power-over".)

4. Who are other Hamans, kings, Esthers, Mordecais, and Vashtis today in our lives? Can you think of types of ordinary people (no names, please!) as well as types of famous ones? (Note: the point of this question is to get at personality differences and differences in the values held by different types of people, not to label or gossip about particular people!)

(K) Write definitions of power with Christian interpretations.

- Say, "In many ways stories in the Old Testament seem to assume that power-over others is a natural thing, that God approves of it, and that God actually uses this method to gain God's own ends. Does Jesus give us the same message about power? Or does Jesus offer more an image of power-with-others?" Invite class members to discuss this a few minutes.
- Then ask each one to write definitions of "power-over" and "power-with."
- After they have had time to write definitions, invite several class members to share their definitions.
- Possible discussion starter: What makes a definition of power "Christian" or "unchristian"?

(L) Paint your feelings about power.

- For this activity you will need paper, paints, brushes, glasses of water (to rinse brushes after each color is used), and newspaper to protect tables. This activity might be offered as class members arrive as a way to get in touch with feelings about power before the whole class discusses the Bible passage.
- Invite persons to create a symbolic picture of how they feel when faced with powerful people and/or systems. Some class members might want to paint two pictures (perhaps by dividing their paper in half). The second picture should symbolize something about their decision of how to act in the face of such power (or perhaps something about their journey toward gaining the strength and resolve to act in the face of people and systems who use "power-over" tactics).
- Ask some class members to share their paintings and any insights they gained about themselves and power.

(M) Reflect on Haman.

- Invite class members to reflect in writing about the following:
—Who are the Hamans in my life?
—Is there any Haman in me (in my use of power and in my approach to other people)?
- After allowing time for class members to write and reflect, invite several to either read an excerpt from their writings or tell some insights they gained about themselves.

(N) Enlist a volunteer for the next session.

- Activity "F" in Chapter 13 will need some advance preparation. (See page 64.) You will need to find a volunteer to read "The Courier's Tale" (page 66) before the next session and to present the story to class members.

Additional Bible Helps

A Look at the Book of Esther as Literature

While sometimes labeled harsh and vindictive, the story of Esther is nevertheless a well-told, fast-paced tale of intrigue, complete with villain, hero, and heroine. The storyteller was an accomplished artist who crafted this story very skillfully, using such literary devices as irony and dramatic reversals. He or she expertly orchestrated coincidences to heighten the suspense. At times Esther has the flavor of a modern melodrama or mystery. As a skillful piece of literature, Esther makes its points—even the religious ones—without being preachy or moralistic in tone.

The story of Esther can be divided into three major sections: the introduction (Chapters 1 and 2); the main plot (Chapters 3 through 8); and the conclusion (Chapter 9).

The Introduction. The storyteller quickly sets the stage. This story takes place in the Persian court of King Ahasuerus. We are introduced to the enormous size of the empire and to the wealth of its king. We also immediately get some important clues about this king: he boasts about his empire, and he and his male cronies are prone to long feasts and drinking events. About his queen, Vashti, we learn little, for the storyteller does not expect her to be around long. We are not to identify with her except to learn the harsh lesson that, if we are women, doing something rash like she did will get us banished forever. We do learn something about the men King Ahasuerus has appointed to give him wise advice: they are manipulators of events to keep the power balance in their favor!

With quick, broad strokes, the storyteller shifts abruptly in Chapter 2 to introduce the hero and heroine of his tale: Mordecai and Esther. Mordecai, a Jew, has a minor post in the Persian court and an adopted daughter who is really his orphaned cousin. Esther, the young orphaned Jew is an obedient, compliant woman who eagerly pleases the men who are guiding her, even to the point of hiding her Jewish religion. We also get a hint of what is to come, for Esther has the commitment to accomplish what she sets out to do: she wins the favor of the eunuch Hegai and the favor of the king, who makes her his new queen. We also get a hint about Esther's approach to power when she reports the assassination plan and gives Mordecai due credit.

The Main Plot. Having quickly set the stage of the tale and introduced three of the four main characters of his story, the storyteller then introduces us to the villain (Haman the Agagite) and to the conflict (Mordecai's refusal to bow down to a descendent of his people's ancient enemy, the Agagites). Haman, a powerful and rather self-centered person, is furious and overreacts. He decides to plot the total annihilation of Jews in Persia as revenge against Mordecai.

There it is. The dynamics are all there now for a good story: a king who is ruled by his passions and who can be manipulated by his trusted servants and his wife; a stubbornly faithful Jew; a rather powerless queen who seems to be totally assimilated into the Persian court and its ways; and a particular servant who has a whole lot of power over other people and a mean streak in his personality! Added to that powerful mix is a crucial fact that our skillful storyteller has allowed only us as readers to know: the new Persian queen is a Jew! Haman, the villain, does not even suspect what he is getting into! The storyteller has set up a situation where ancient Jewish readers would surely be questioning:

—Who will save our people?

—Who will save the queen?

—How will God intervene on behalf of his chosen people?

—Is this a story where the Jews prevail or a story where God "teaches Jews a lesson" because we have been unfaithful? (Remember, Jews in the Persian Empire after the Exile had other storytellers who used Hebrew history to make a point about God's demands and the people's faithfulness or lack of it. They had heard the stories of the Deuteronomistic storyteller and the Chronicler.)

Once the villain is introduced in Chapter 3, the storyteller uses a quick series of coincidences and reversals to bring the tale to its climax: the king cannot sleep, so he reads the royal court records and is reminded about Mordecai's previous loyalty. Haman thinks the king is going to honor him, only to discover that it is his enemy Mordecai the king wants to honor. Haman manipulates the king into allowing the decree to kill all the Jews only to have Mordecai and Esther outwit him. Esther takes power and manipulates the king and Haman into a lovely set of banquets and then lowers the boom on Haman. Esther and Mordecai shrewdly counteract Haman's decree with one of their own. "Ah," readers then and now say, "the threat against the Jews has been averted; God's hand has been in this all along; the chosen people are saved."

The Conclusion. But wait, the storyteller is not finished. Esther and Mordecai's decree allowed the Jews to arm themselves and mount a defense against any armed forces who sought to kill them. Quietly, the storyteller announces that Haman's allies have deserted him, Persians are claiming to be Jews, many are fearful of Mordecai's power; and on the fateful day, not one Persian raises arms against the Jews. "Whew," we say, "that's the end! The killing has been averted."

Not so, says the storyteller. The Jews rise up all over the Persian Empire and slaughter thousands of their enemies. Esther pleads with the king for a second day of slaughter and gets it. More Persian enemies are killed.

Finally, our storyteller tells his readers: After all the killing, the Jews feasted. That feast is called *Purim* (or "the day of Mordecai"). You Jewish readers are to hold the feast of Purim each year in memory of the day "the Jews gained relief from their enemies" (9:22).

"What is this?" readers ask. "Who told this story, and why?" Was this really a Jewish storyteller pointing out how God saves his people? Was it a kind of coded "pep talk" story told to Jews in a time when they were being badly persecuted, a time when hatred of enemies was great enough that those first readers/listeners would have tolerated even unprovoked mass slaughter? Was it an anti-Jewish story told by pagans who gave the characters the names of the god Marduk and the goddess Ishtar and made it seem like a Jewish story? Why did the story end this way?

Looked at from a literary standpoint, Esther is like many really great stories: It leaves much unsaid and allows the reader to draw his or her own conclusions!

13

"For Such a Time as This"

Esther 9:1-23

LEARNING MENU

Keeping in mind the ways your class members learn best, as well as their needs and interests, choose at least one learning segment from each of the three Dimensions.

Dimension 1: What Does the Bible Say?

(A) Count the feasts in Esther.

- Ask class members to skim through the Book of Esther to discover how many feasts are mentioned in the story of Esther and what different purposes they serve. Ask them to prepare a short report.
- Note: Feasts are mentioned in: 1:5; 1:9; 2:18; 5:5; 7:1; 8:17; 9:17; and 9:18.

(B) Research Purim and other Jewish festivals.

- Ask class members to look up in a Bible dictionary *feasts, festivals,* and *fasting* (or some variation of those words) to discover the ancient Jewish festivals. Suggest that they especially look for information on Purim (which may have its own separate listing in a Bible dictionary).
- Ask them to prepare a short report on: What are the main Jewish festivals, and what historical events do they commemorate?

(C) Find out why there was no plundering by the Jews.

- Ask class members to review Haman's edict (3:13), Mordecai and Esther's edict (8:11), and what actually happened (9:6-10, 14-16). Have them explore the following two questions:
  1. What does each passage say about plundering?
  2. Why did the Jews not plunder their enemies' goods?
- Note: The lack of plundering by the Jews is sometimes pointed to as justification for the killing that took place. The lack of plundering, say some scholars and commentators, means the Jews were fighting for survival of their people, not for increased wealth and not for revenge; that made the killings acceptable. The emphasis on lack of plundering may also be a reference to the Agag story in 1 Samuel 15:9 where Saul and his people destroyed almost everything of Agag's and took the rest as sacrifice to God.

(D) Discover what almost kept Esther from getting into the Bible.

- You will need several commentaries on Esther and the Additions to Esther, along with a study Bible that has the Apocrypha included in it. Hang up the chart class members made in activity "C," Chapter 11.
- Remind class members that the Book of Esther had a hard time getting accepted as part of the official "canon" of the Bible. Provide them with commentaries and Bible dictionaries, and ask them to explore the reasons ancient religious leaders did not want it in the Bible. What or who helped it get into the Bible? How did the Greek Additions to Esther help it? (Explore particularly the dream of Mordecai and its interpretation—Additions A and F—which put God and divine providence into the story.)

(E) Review the questions in the study book.

- If some class members have not completed the questions in their study books, give them time to do so when they arrive in class. Other students can work on activities "A"—"D."
- Review the answers to the questions quickly and move on to activities in Dimension 2 and 3.
- Suggested answers:
  1. The enemies of the Jews (Persians whom Haman had rallied with his edict) became fearful when Haman was killed and Mordecai was promoted to Haman's position. They probably also were fearful as they saw how much influence Queen Esther had over the king.
  2. Scripture does not specifically say that the enemies of the Jews raised arms against the Jews. However, it does not specifically say they did not, either. (The Persian court of Ahasuerus's time was relatively tolerant of the Jews who had earlier been deported into Babylon—by this time part of the Persian Empire. The story of Esther, though it takes place in Ahasuerus's time, may actually have been written at a later time when Jews were being persecuted.)
  3. The Jews carry out a systematic slaughter of their enemies (but remember there is no independent, historical evidence that this massive killing ever took place).
  4. The Jews feasted after the days of killing. (Whether that feast was an entirely new one or some kind of feast day already established in Persia, we do not know. Some have speculated that the feast was originally a New Year's festival in ancient Persia that the Jews in exile adopted. According to this theory the story of Esther then was written to remake the feast day into a Jewish one. Since many of the Jewish festivals are based on remembrance of historical events, the Jewish festival of Purim was so named after Haman's casting of lots in a plot to kill the Jews in Persia.) Mordecai urges the Jews to keep this festival each year. In verses 29-32, Queen Esther also urges the Jews to keep the festival of Purim.

Dimension 2: What Does the Bible Mean?

(F) Experience "The Courier's Tale."

- Before class time invite one of the men of the class to prepare the story of "The Courier's Tale" ("Additional Bible Helps," page 66). If he can, ask him to learn it well enough to tell it rather than read it.
- Tell class members that ancient Persia had a famous courier postal system (that was similar to the Pony Express in pioneer days in the United States). Invite them to get comfortable and to listen to a tale told by one of those Persian couriers of King Ahasuerus's court.
- Ask for the storyteller to present "The Courier's Tale."
- If you have time, after hearing "The Courier's Tale" ask each class member to write a similar "tale" about Esther and Mordecai's actions and their decree. Assign each class member a different identity from which to tell their tale: a maid of Esther's, a servant of the king's, Haman's wife, a Jewish man in Susa, a Jewish woman in Susa, a Jew in an outlying province, a child in Susa, and so on. What would each of them have to say about what happened to Haman and what was about to happen next?
- After they have had time to write their tales, bring them all together and let them read their tales quickly one after another.
- Then ask what insights they gained into the story of Esther by thinking about the events from another person's point of view.

(G) Examine hard questions.

- Use the following questions as discussion starters about the meaning of the end of Esther.
  1. How does the storyteller seem to interpret and justify the mass killings in Chapter 9?
  2. Even though the direct evidence of God is scant in the story, does divine guidance seem to be operating here in ways we have previously seen in Kings and Chronicles?
  3. How does the storyteller seem to portray Esther and her decision to have the enemies of the Jews killed? Does the storyteller place any moral judgment on Esther's decisions?
  4. Do you agree or disagree with the idea in the study

book that the storyteller seems to "demilitarize" the end of the story by jumping quickly to the celebration and its establishment as an annual festival? What evidence, if any, can you point to in Chapter 9 of Esther to support your point of view?

(H) Review the Kings—Esther history.

- If you have been making a wall timeline throughout this unit of study, use it with this activity.
- Tell class members: "We are now completing the thirteen sessions on the biblical story of the Hebrews. Our story began with King Solomon in 961 B.C. Our story ends (at least in this quarter) with the tale of Esther, a Jew who lived in Persia in 483 B.C. We have covered almost five hundred years of Jewish history."
- Invite class members to call out the three most crucial events of that five-hundred-year period. Then ask them to summarize the one or two most important messages from that five-hundred-year story of Israel.
  Note: There is no absolutely right answer here.
- Possible events:
—division of the monarchy
—the Exile
—the return to Jerusalem
- Possible messages:
—God has a plan for his chosen people and rewards them when they are faithful and punishes them when they are unfaithful;
—People, events, and systems can work with the divine plan for justice or against it; actions have consequences that (like the Exile) are sometimes global and devastating; but there is always another choice, another decision to make about how to live faithfully.

Dimension 3: What Does the Bible Mean to Us?

(J) Engage in a "relay" debate on violence and change.

- You will need to print on the board or newsprint the quotation from Bankson (see below) so that class members will be able to see it and refer to it during this activity. Also provide several sheets of newsprint and markers for the two groups to use.
- Tell class members: "Marjory Bankson, in her book *Braided Streams: Esther and a Woman's Way of Growing*, says: 'When we confront a system based on violence, then violence will be part of a change as the old order struggles to maintain control' " (LuraMedia, 1985; page 153).
- Divide class members into two groups: One group is to list all the reasons and evidence they can think of to support this statement. The other group is to list all the reasons and evidence they can think of to refute or disprove the statement.
- Engage in a "relay debate": Place two chairs at the front of the room, facing each other. When the groups have their arguments and evidence ready, ask them to post their sheets of newsprint so they will be able to see them and then to form two lines (like a relay race) facing the two chairs. Give the teams the following rules: "When I blow the whistle/call time/say go, the first member of each team quickly takes a seat and starts the debate about the quotation. After two minutes, I will blow the whistle again/call time/say stop, which means 'next person takes the chair and continues the debate where the previous person left off.' The question to be debated is: Is the quote from Bankson true or false?"
- When the relay is over, gather class members together and discuss the following question: Is there any other way to move from a system that includes violence to a system that is based on peace?

(J) Reflect on "being called to a time such as this."

- Ask class members to review the decision that Esther had to make in 4:13-14 and how she carried out her decision. This review might be done verbally by the whole class.
- Then invite each person to reflect in writing on the questions:
—Have you ever felt you were called to do something for a particular time or reason?
—How was your situation like or unlike Esther's?
- Note: If persons say they cannot think of anything in their life like that, ask them to write about what such a call might look like in their future.
- When participants have had time to write, invite several to share excerpts or insights they gained from writing about this topic.

(K) Engage in more discussion.

- Use the following as possible discussion starters for Dimension 3 in the study book.
  1. What is "providence"? How does the storyteller of Esther portray it? How would you describe divine providence or divine will today? (See "Additional Bible Helps," "The Point of Esther," page 67.)
  2. One commentator says that God is present in Esther's very weakness and powerlessness. Do you agree or disagree? Why?
  3. Is violence ever justified?

4. Is Esther a shrewd manipulator, a faithful Jew, or both?

(L) Write a belief statement about God's will.

- Individually or in teams of two write short "belief" statements about providence. In particular, urge persons to deal with these questions:
—How do you answer the big WHY? questions of life?
—What part does God play in human decisions and tragedies?
- After class members have had time to write statements, invite several to read theirs aloud. Invite the whole group to reflect on how their various statements are similar to one another's or how they illustrate different ways to think about divine providence. Be sure to affirm each person's belief statement as being valid for him or her. No one has the ultimate right answer here except God!

(M) Create a banner "for such a time as this."

- For this activity you will need art materials, scissors, glue or other adherent, and either lengths of cloth or pieces of poster board to make banners. If your group is small, all class members might work together to create one banner.
- Ask class members to brainstorm for a few minutes about symbols and images that could be used to represent the thought "Perhaps you have come to royal dignity for such a time as this." The banner or banners might use the whole statement or just the words "for such a time as this" or perhaps a modern variation such as "called for just this reason."
- Remember, banners usually have just one point and few words. They may use one or more symbols to convey the idea.

(N) Participate in a closing worship.

- To close this unit of study of First Kings through Esther, ask class members to use a litany or prayer written in earlier sessions. Or perhaps they could at this time write a closing prayer that reflects the insights and concerns of this whole study of Kings through Esther.
- This worship might be planned before class time by two or three students, or it might be planned by several students who arrive early for the class session. The banner (see activity "M" above) can serve as a focal point for the closing worship time.

Additional Bible Helps

The Courier's Tale
By Johanna Bos

"I tell you, it is becoming a bit much. When I took the job, they told me I wouldn't have to go out too often, and the pay was good. But here I am, back on a horse riding for all I'm worth through all the provinces. Everything in a hurry, no time for a good night's sleep. And in every town the whole proclamation needs to be cried out. Every time, I need to find a crier and most of the time an interpreter. I am good and sick of it, I can tell you. What does it say? Well, I suppose I can give you the gist of it. It isn't secret after all. But let's sit down then, they just have to wait a bit for the news in the next province. And I could do with a rest.

"You know the story of Haman? You don't? Where have you been? I thought everyone knew. Anyway, to make a long story short, he was the king's advisor and had it in for the Jews. He was going to have them done away with once and for all and was willing to pay money to have it done. That was the message I went out with the last time; and the time before that, it was Vashti. It has been one commotion after another in this kingdom. Anyway, they say that Haman finally stepped on the king's toes, tried to molest the queen, in the palace no less. I'm only telling you what they told me. But I have it from a good source, a serving woman in the palace told me what went on that night. They hadn't seen the king so mad since that business with Vashti. Practically foaming at the mouth, he was. Luckily, there were some folk around who pointed out a quick solution to the problem. Before he knew it, Haman was squirming from the noose he had ready for someone else. A fine sight that must have been.

"The thing of it is, nobody could quite figure out how the queen was going to get the Jews out of the mess they were in. Once the king's edict had gone out, there was no recalling it, you see. Oh, that you do know. So, as you understand, the king couldn't solve it either: he had to stick to that law himself. So, he told Queen Esther and her cousin, Mordecai I believe is his name, to put their heads together, and they could use his authority to enforce whatever they came up with. No one can say that the queen isn't smart; she plays the king like a fiddle, they say.

"Anyway, where was I? Oh yes, what she and Mordecai came up with is this: On the day that the hunt is up, in Adar, the Jews are allowed to defend themselves, meet the hunters armed so to speak. They have permission to do to others what the others would do to them. If that isn't clever, I would like to know what is.

"What did you say? Yeah, like as not, no one will go after them under those circumstances. A real opportunity for peace here. I don't know though, it isn't the way people are, if you know what I mean. There are quite a few around who are spoiling for a fight. They were looking forward to doing openly what they had been doing for so long on the sly.

"Then there are those who pretend that they belong to the Jews themselves. That is the greatest sight, to see them scurrying around looking for the proper way to behave, to follow the customs of the Jews. It is going to be something, I tell you. But I'm not in charge of that, I only need to get ten more letters delivered and seen to. Better get moving, nice talking with you!"

From *Ruth and Esther: Women in Alien Lands*, by Johanna W. H. Bos; Mission Education and Cultivation Program Department for The Women's Division, General Board of Global Ministries, The United Methodist Church, 1987; pages 77–8; used by permission of the author.

The Point of Esther
What is the main point of Esther? What was the storyteller trying to say to his first readers? What does it mean to us today? Here's what several different scholars say about Esther:

• "The novella is designed to entertain and show how humans act under certain circumstances" (*Harper's Bible Dictionary*; page 280).

• "The Book of Esther shows us that the Jews of the Diaspora—i.e. those Jews who did *not* return to Jerusalem following Cyrus' decree—were still counted as God's people and had a role to play in the future of the whole" (*Ezra, Nehemiah, and Esther: The Daily Study Bible Series*, J. G. McConville; Westminster, 1985; page 152).

• "Esther is the fascinating tale that provides the 'historical' basis for a non-Mosaic (and, probably, originally a pagan) festival. . . . The book has frequently been faulted for its moral tone. . . . Nonetheless, Esther is still a religious work. For although the Deity is not seen or even heard on its stage, God is standing in the wings, following the drama and arranging the props for a successful resolution of the play. . . . Providence can be relied upon to reverse the ill-fortunes that beset individuals or the nation—provided that such leaders and their followers actively do their part, acting wisely and courageously. . . . [Esther combines] a harem tale involving a certain Vashti, a court intrigue/deliverance tale featuring a Mordecai, a success/deliverance tale starring an Esther. . ." (*The New Oxford Annotated Bible [New Revised Standard Version]*, edited by Bruce M. Metzeger and Roland E. Murphy; Oxford University Press, 1991; page 612OT).

• "[Esther is] . . . an account of the trials and triumphs of figures involved in intrigues in foreign courts (see Gen 39–41; Dan 1–6) . . . Coincidences (or possibly providence) combine with human initiative to bring about a resolution in which good triumphs over evil. . . . Readers experience the universe as ultimately just, a satisfaction real life rarely provides" (*Harper/Collins Study Bible*, Wayne A. Meeks, general editor; Harper/Collins Publishers, 1993; pages 736–37).

• "Esther is a book peculiar to Jewish history, which celebrates the survival of the Jewish people by means of a woman's intercession." This author says we must read Esther in light of the oppression of Jews in second/first century B.C. for that is when the story was likely finalized. Those under persecution are often helped by the act of mocking their oppressors (Johanna Bos, *Ruth and Esther: Women in Alien Lands;* General Board of Global Ministries, The United Methodist Church; pages 40, 39).

• Sidnie Ann White notes that male Protestant Christian scholars downplayed Esther and made Mordecai the hero and the brains of the strategy to save the Jews; Esther just obeyed Mordecai's directions (*Women's Bible Commentary*, page 126).

Two Histories of Israel

By Mary Jo Osterman

How is the Bible put together? Well, there is the Old Testament and the New Testament. The Old Testament has three major sections: the Law, the Prophets, and the Writings. The New Testament has the Gospels and Acts, the letters of Paul and others, and Revelation.

The above description summarizes in very general terms how we have traditionally described the outline of the Bible. The Old Testament description comes from the Hebrew organization of the Bible. While this makes good sense in some ways, it also creates problems. For example, it does not make a lot of sense to include the historical books of Joshua through Kings with the prophets. Also, it is hard to place First and Second Chronicles, Ezra–Nehemiah, and Esther in the traditional outline.

For these and other reasons, biblical scholar David Clines offers us another way to divide and group the first seventeen books of the Old Testament. His scheme places our biblical material in a helpful larger context:

"The books Genesis to Esther are the narrative books of the O[ld] T[estament]. Together they contain two distinct story sequences, which are alike in many ways but which also show surprising and important differences. The first narrative sequence, which may be called the Primary History, runs from Genesis to 2 Kings, and the second, the Secondary History, from 1 Chronicles to Esther" (*Harper's Bible Commentary*, James L. Mays, general editor; Harper & Row, 1988; page 74).

The Primary History of Israel

The primary history of Israel begins with the Book of Genesis and ends with the end of the second book of Kings. It begins with the story of creation and ends with the people of Israel in Exile in 587/586 B.C. The last story in Second Kings about Jehoiachin being released from prison probably occurred around 561 B.C.—which means the final version of the Book of Kings—and the final version of the primary history—was not written before 561 B.C.

This twelve-book primary history of Israel has a single editorial and theological point of view. Biblical scholars have identified it as the Deuteronomistic historian's viewpoint since the writer or writers of this history viewed everything from the perspective of the Book of Deuteronomy. The Deuteronomist evaluated Israel's history on the basis of whether and how Israel followed "the laws of Moses" as set forth in the Book of Deuteronomy, especially Chapters 12 through 26. Because Israel did not live up to those laws, the primary history, says Clines, "consistently stresses elements of decline, disaster, and failure in the national history" (*Harper's Bible Commentary*, page 74). This history is a story of "fair beginnings and foul endings" (*Harper's Bible Commentary*, page 75).

The Secondary History of Israel

The secondary history of Israel begins with First Chronicles and ends with Esther, says Clines. It also opens with creation. However, creation is told through a long list of "begats," which tells the genealogy of the people from Adam and Eve onward. The secondary history tells the story of the kings, but from the Chronicler's point of view. It also tells about the end of exile and the rebuilding of Jerusalem (Ezra–Nehemiah). This history of Israel ends with a story of some of the people who are still living outside Jerusalem, under Persian rule (Esther). Specifically it ends with Mordecai being installed as a Jewish prime minister in the mid-400's B.C.

The secondary history of Israel, says Clines, "emphasizes positive aspects" of Israel's history rather than the decline and downfall (*Harper's Bible Commentary*, page 74). The books in this secondary history, though perhaps not written by the same person, all come from the same literary and religious circle which scholars identify as "the Chronicler."

An Invitation to Us

These two histories are laid next to each other in our Bible without explanation or comment. We are thus invited in every generation to assess their significance. We are invited to examine for ourselves what constitutes success or failure of the Israelite people and what constitutes blessing or curse, promise and fulfillment from God. We are invited by the Bible to decide whether the Exile was God's punishment for abandoning faith in Yahweh or for desecrating the Temple or whether perhaps the Exile had another meaning altogether.

This article is a summary of David J. A. Clines's article "Introduction to the Biblical Story: Genesis–Esther" in *Harper's Bible Commentary*, James L. Mays, general editor; HarperSanFrancisco, 1988; pages 74–84.

TWO HISTORIES OF ISRAEL

Primary History Written by Deuteronomistic Historians	Secondary History Written by Chronicler Historians
Genesis	1 Chronicles
Exodus	2 Chronicles
Leviticus	Ezra
Numbers	Nehemiah
Deuteronomy	Esther
Joshua	
Judges	
Ruth	
1 Samuel	
2 Samuel	
1 Kings	
2 Kings	

The First Audiences

By Mary Jo Osterman

The Audience of the Deuteronomistic Storytellers
The kings of the monarchy lived from 1020 (Saul) to 560/later B.C. (Jehoiachin), but scholars agree that the final version of Kings, the version we basically have today, was written during the Exile in Babylonia by a storyteller who lived sometime after 561 B.C. since he knew what had happened to Jehoiachin in Babylonia (2 Kings 25:27). His audience was a mix of people: some who were in exile in Babylonia; others who were left on the conquered land; and still others who had fled to Egypt.

Those in Exile in Babylonia
We are told in Second Kings that the conquerors (Assyria and then Babylonia) deported thousands of people from Israel in the north and from Judah in the south. The kings were either killed or deported, the religious leaders (priests and prophets) were deported. The people were first put into agricultural internment settlements (Ezekiel 3:15) where they built houses and farmed. Because of limited resources, leaders seemed to scramble for their own interests (Ezekiel 34:1-10). However, the people in exile enjoyed relative prosperity and eventually began to enter the world of commerce. To keep their religious/national identity and set themselves apart from their pagan neighbors, they began to practice sabbath-keeping and circumcision.

Those Left in Judah/Israel
Some biblical scholars believe that the storyteller who lived during the Exile spoke not only to those who lived in Babylonia, but also to those who were left in the destroyed kingdoms of Judah and Israel.

Only the poorest people were left on the land of the old monarchy to be vinedressers and farmers for their conquerors. The social class system was thus upset. Serious hunger faced the people on the land in early years and those in control of storehouses gained influence. In addition, the conquerors imported into Israel and Judah peoples they had conquered elsewhere. The mix of religious practices became even more pronounced (2 Kings 17:5-6, 24; 24:14; 25:12).

Those Who Fled to Egypt
When Judah was conquered and the people were deported in 587/586 B.C., the king of Babylonia set up a native governor over Judah, which should have meant peace for the people who were left on the land. However, the governor Gedaliah was assassinated by fanatics, and the people fled to Egypt in fear (2 Kings 25:22-26). Even before the Exile, however, a Jewish colony had settled in Egypt, which was very much a cosmopolitan nation.

The First Audience of Kings
Since some biblical scholars believe that the first storyteller of Kings lived before the Exile (before 587/586 B.C.), the first audience would be the people of Judah who still lived in the Southern Kingdom after the Northern Kingdom was gone. They probably lived during King Josiah's time, in 640 to 609, which was three hundred years or so after Solomon reigned. Their storyteller probably told them the stories of the kings up to their time as a warning to them that they needed to reform their ways or what happened to the people of Israel in the Northern Kingdom would happen to them too.

Material for the description of the three exiled communities is based on *First and Second Kings. Interpretation: A Bible Commentary for Teaching and Preaching*, by Richard Nelson; James L. Mays, series editor; John Knox Press, 1987; pages 4–8.]

The Audience of the Chronicler Storyteller
Tradition says that the Chronicler was a Levite or priest living in in the 400's B.C. Scholars indicate the existence of a "priestly circle" of writers who may have written over several centuries, similar to the Deuteronomistic historians; and the books of Chronicles, Ezra-Nehemiah, and Esther show evidence of having been edited and added to by later writers who had more or different information.

Even with imprecise dating, we can tell from the books of Chronicles and Ezra-Nehemiah that the audience was composed of people who lived after the Exile.

One interesting note is that the Book of Chronicles seems not to have the anti-Samaritan (anti-Northern Kingdom) emphasis that Ezra-Nehemiah has. This may be a clue that the audiences were not the same: that the writer of Chronicles may have lived and written right at the beginning of the return to Jerusalem and that the writer or writers of Ezra-Nehemiah lived and wrote later when the tensions among the peoples living in Judah were higher and when a greater threat existed to the purity of Israel's religion.

In any case the writer or writers of the Chronicler circle were writing to people who had been exiled and who had now returned to Jerusalem to rebuild their identity.

SUGGESTED RESOURCE LIST

Braided Streams: Esther and a Woman's Way of Growing, by Marjory Zoet Bankson (LuraMedia, 1985) ISBN 0-931055-05-9.

Chronicles One and *Chronicles Two: Anchor Bible Series*, Volumes 12 and 13, by Jacob M. Myers (Doubleday, 1965); Volume 12, ISBN 0-385-01259-4; Volume 13, ISBN 0-385-03757-0.

Ezra, Nehemiah, and Esther. The Daily Study Bible Series, by J. G. McConville (St. Andrew, Scotland, 1993); ISBN 0-7152-0527-7.

Ezra-Nehemiah. Interpretation: A Bible Commentary for Teaching and Preaching, by Mark A. Throntveit (John Knox, 1992); ISBN 0-8042-3111-7.

First and Second Kings. Interpretation: A Bible Commentary for Teaching and Preaching, by Richard Nelson (John Knox Press, 1987); ISBN 0-8042-31109-5.

First Kings: New Century Bible Commentary, by G. H. Jones (Eerdmans, 1984); ISBN 0-8028-0019-x.

Harper's Bible Commentary, James L. Mays, general editor (HarperSanFrancisco, 1988); ISBN 0-06-065541-0.

Harper's Bible Dictionary, Paul J. Achtemeier, general editor (HarperSanFrancisco, 1985); ISBN 0-06-069862-4.

The Interpreter's Bible, Volume 3, Kings–Job; George A. Buttrick, editor (Abingdon Press, 1954); ISBN 0-687-19209-9.

The Interpreter's One-Volume Commentary of the Bible, edited by Charles M. Laymon (Abingdon Press, 1971); ISBN 0-687-19299-4.

I & II Chronicles: The Daily Study Bible Series, by J. G. McConville (St. Andrew Scotland, 1993); ISBN 0-7152-0527-7.

Ruth and Esther: Women in Alien Lands, by Johanna Bos (Mission Education and Cultivation Program Department, The Women's Division, General Board of Global Ministries, The United Methodist Church; 1987).

Second Kings: New Century Bible Commentary, by G. H. Jones (Eerdmans, 1984); ISBN 0-8028-0040-8.

The Storyteller's Companion to the Bible, Michael E. Williams, editor (Abingdon Press); Volume 3: *Judges–Kings* (1992, ISBN 0-687-39672-7); Volume 4: *Old Testament Women* (1993, ISBN 0-687-39674-3).

The Women's Bible Commentary, Carol A. Newsom and Sharon H. Ringe, editors (Westminster/John Knox, 1992); ISBN 0-664-21922-5). See especially Kings, Chronicles, Ezra-Nehemiah, Esther entries.

WomanWisdom and *WomanWitness: Women of the Hebrew Scriptures, Parts One and Two*, by Miriam Therese Winter (Crossroad); Part One (1991, ISBN 0-8245-1100-x); Part Two (1991, ISBN 0-8245-1141-7).

CHRONOLOGY CHART FOR KINGS THROUGH ESTHER

UNITED KINDGOM OF ISRAEL	
1020–1000	Saul
1000–961	David
961–922	Solomon
	Bathsheba, Queen Mother

JUDAH	
922–915	Rehoboam, Solomon's son
915–873	Two more kings
873–849	Jehoshaphat
849–842	Two more kings
842–837	Athaliah, only ruling queen
837–715	Five more kings
715–687	Hezekiah, a faithful king
687–640	Two more kings
640–609	Josiah, a faithful king
	Huldah, prophetess in Judah 609–598
	Two more kings
598–597	Jehoiachin, three months
	First Deportation to Babylonia
597–587	Zedekiah
587–586	*Fall of Jerusalem and Temple in Southern Kingdom and Second Deportation to Babylonia*

ISRAEL	
922–901	Jeroboam I
	Ahijah, prophet in Israel
901–869	Five kings
869–850	Ahab and Queen Jezebel
	Elijah, prophet in Israel
850–732	Eleven more kings
	Book of First Kings ends: Ahaziah ruling
732–721	Hoshea
722–721	*Fall of Samaria and the Northern Kingdom of Israel*

EXILE	
560	Jehoiachin released from prison in Babylonia
	Book of Second Kings ends
	The Deuteronomist historian writes final version of Book of Kings

RETURN FROM EXILE AND DIASPORA JEWS	
538	The edict of Cyrus /First Return and reconstruction of the Temple begins
520–515	Second Return/Temple completed
486–464	King Xerxes I rules Persian empire Esther takes place
483	Story of Esther takes place
458	Third Return/Ezra takes the Law back to Jerusalem (alternative date: 427–397)
445-433	Fourth Return/Nehemiah rebuilds walls of Jerusalem
c. 400	Memoirs of Ezra and Nehemiah were combined in one document
300's–100's	Book of Esther and Additions written
c. 300	Book of Ezra-Nehemiah completed

Note: All dates given are "B.C.," or "Before Christ." The abbreviation *c.* before a date stands for the Latin word *circa*, which means "approximately."

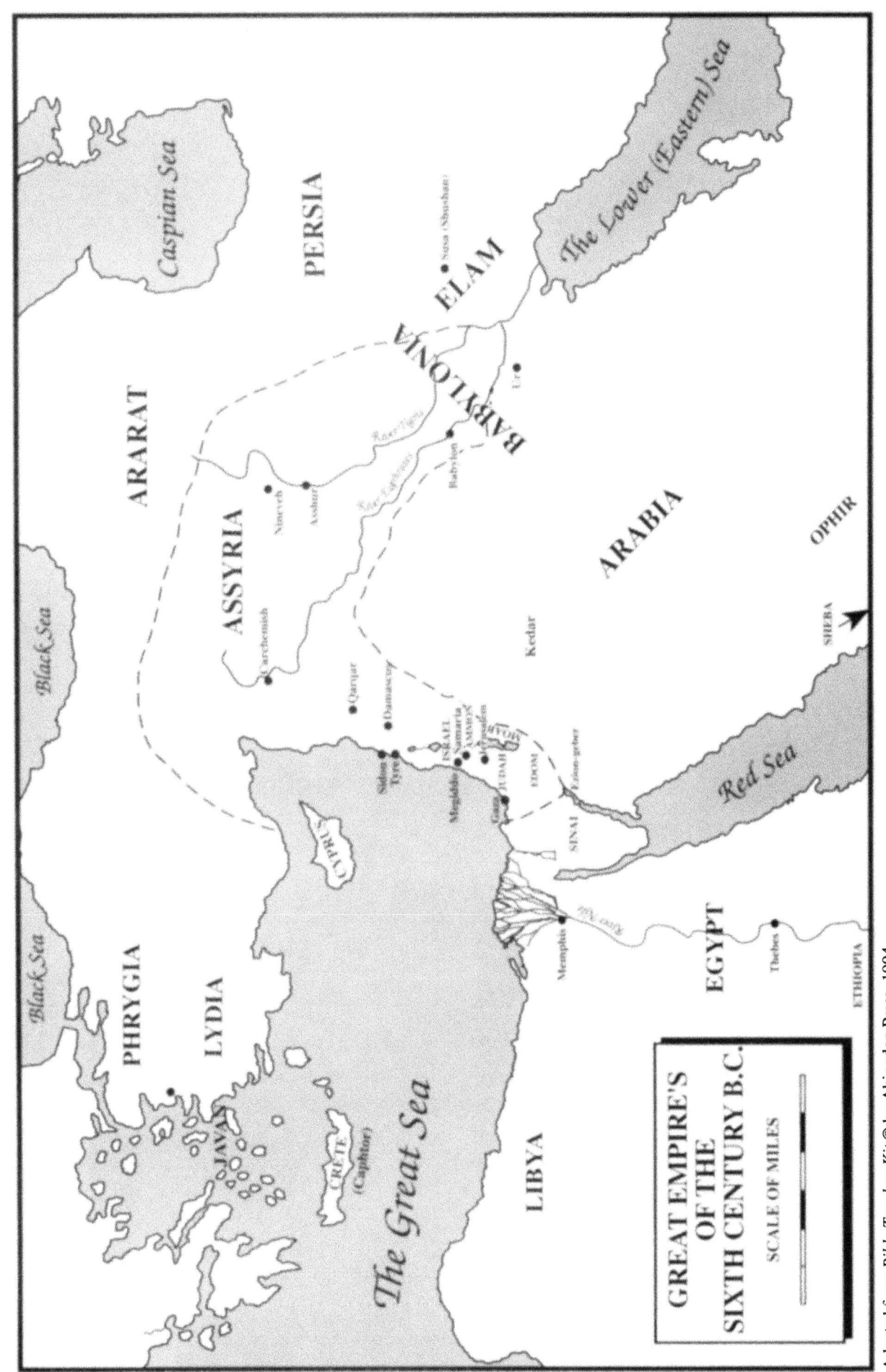

Adapted from *Bible Teacher Kit* © by Abingdon Press, 1994

www.ingramcontent.com/pod-product-compliance
Lightning Source LLC
LaVergne TN
LVHW061316060426
835507LV00019B/2173